The Griesbach Hypothesis
and Redaction Criticism

THE SOCIETY OF BIBLICAL LITERATURE
MONOGRAPH SERIES

Adela Yarbro Collins, Editor
E. F. Campbell, Associate Editor

Number 41
THE GRIESBACH HYPOTHESIS
AND REDACTION CRITICISM

by
Sherman E. Johnson

Sherman E. Johnson

THE GRIESBACH HYPOTHESIS
AND REDACTION CRITICISM

Scholars Press
Atlanta, Georgia

THE GRIESBACH HYPOTHESIS
AND REDACTION CRITICISM

by
Sherman E. Johnson

©1991
The Society of Biblical Literature

Library of Congress Cataloging in Publication Data

Johnson, Sherman E. (Sherman Elbridge), 1908-
    The Griesbach hypothesis and redaction criticism / Sherman E.
    Johnson.
    p. cm. — (Monograph series / the Society of Biblical
    Literature ; no. 41)
    Includes bibliographical references and index.
    ISBN 1-55540-532-0 (alk. paper). — ISBN 1-55540-533-9 (alk.
    paper)
    1. Griesbach hypothesis (Synoptics criticism) 2. Bible. N.T.
Gospels—Criticism, Redaction. 3. Bible. N.T. Mark—Criticism,
Redaction. I. Title. II. Series: Monograph series (Society of Biblical
Literature) ; no. 41.
BS2555.2.J64   1990
226'.066—dc20
                                90-44913
                                CIP

Printed in the United States of America
on acid-free paper

CONTENTS

ABBREVIATIONS

GH	Griesbach Hypothesis
2DH	Two Document Hypothesis (Mark and Q)
AJT	*American Journal of Theology*
ATR	*Anglican Theological Review*
BETL	*Bibliotheca ephemeridium theologicarum lovaniensium*
EvT	*Evangelische Theologie*
HTR	*Harvard Theological Review*
IB	*Interpreter's Bible*
IDB	*Interpreter's Dictionary of the Bible* (4 vols. and Supplementary Vol.)
JAAR	*Journal of the American Academy of Religion*
JBL	*Journal of Biblical Literature*
JR	*Journal of Religion*
JTS	*Journal of Theological Studies*
m	mishna
NovT	*Novum Testamentum*
NTAbh	*Neutestamentiche Abhandlungen*
NTS	*New Testament Studies*
PCB	*Peake's Commentary on the Bible*
SBLDS	*Society of Biblical Literature Dissertation Series*

Introduction

The hypothesis of J. J. Griesbach, that Matthew is the earliest gospel, that Luke made use of Matthew. and that Mark is dependent on both, was revived by William R. Farmer more than twenty years ago.[1] Although the priority of Mark and the Two-Document hypothesis (2DH) continue to be defended, and many New Testament specialists accept it as "an assured result of criticism,"[2] Farmer's restatement of the Griesbach hypothesis (GH) has a number of followers. Prior to Farmer's work there were scholars in this century who considered Matthew the earliest gospel and rejected the hypothesis of a Q document,[3] but Farmer has made a case for the GH that should not be ignored, and he has several followers, notably T. R. W. Longstaff, Dom Bernard Orchard, and D. L. Dungan.[4]

---

[1] W. R. Farmer, *The Synoptic Problem: A Critical Analysis* (New York: Macmillan, 1964). The second edition (Dillsboro, NC: Western North Carolina Press 1976) is a reprint with very few changes. See especially 228, where Farmer withdrew his previous argument that "there was a tendency for the gospel tradition to become more specific." In a letter to me, Prof. Edward C. Hobbs reminds me that the GH should really be called the Owen hypothesis, since it was first put forth by Robert Owen in 1764. Farmer does indeed mention Owen, 7, n. 8. The 2DH goes back to C. H. Weisse (17).

[2] See, e.g., G. M. Styler in C. F. Moule, *The Birth of the New Testament* (London: Black, 1962) 223–32; J. A. Fitzmyer, *To Advance the Gospel* (New York: Crossroad, 1981) 3-40; A. M. Honoré, "A Statistical Study of the Synoptic Problem," *NovT* 10 (1968) 95–147. In the opinion of Honoré, Mark is the earliest gospel; next to Mark, Matthew is the most likely candidate. The fullest statistical discussion is that of Robert Morgenthaler, *Statistische Synopse* (Zurich and Stuttgart: Gotthelf, 1971).

[3] E.g., B. C. Butler, *The Originality of St. Matthew* (Cambridge: Cambridge University Press, 1951); A. M. Farrer, "On Dispensing with Q," *Studies in the Gospels* (ed. D. E. Nineham; Cambridge: Cambridge University Press, 1951) 55–58.

[4] A full bibliography to about 1982 is given by C. M. Tuckett, *The Revival of the Griesbach Hypothesis: An Analysis and Appraisal* (Cambridge: Cambridge University Press, 1983). A convenient collection of articles for and against the priority of Mark

There have been some answers to Farmer, e.g., by Talbert and McKnight, but the most comprehensive criticism of his book is that of Tuckett.[5] This British scholar is careful not to claim too much. After saying in his conclusion that the 2DH provides a better explanation of the phenomena, he adds, "Clearly Luke and Mark could have done what the hypothesis claims; what is still lacking is a detailed explanation of why they might have done this."[6]

Farmer himself has realized that it is necessary to face this question. Toward the end of his book he suggests that Mark's work has a cultic orientation "in which an account of the Gospel was formulated in such a way as to bring worshipers hearing it read in church to a fever point of eschatological expectation precisely at the point where Mark began his account of the Passion narrative."[7] He adds two other points. (1) Mark would be useful where a shorter version of the Gospel was more practical; (2) it was suitable for "mixed" congregations including Christians who had come from different places where different gospels were read in church, i.e. as compared with Matthew and Luke it was more neutral [8]

If the discussion is to be carried on fruitfully, it is my conviction that one must consider the setting in life of Mark's gospel from the point of view of the GH, comparing this with the setting now advanced by the majority of scholars, and to take into account the theologies of all three

---

and the Q hypothesis is brought together in A. J. Bellinzoni and others (eds.), *The Two-Source Hypothesis: A Critical Appraisal* (Macon, GA: Mercer University Press, 1965). This includes articles by Styler, Fitzmyer, and Farrer in notes 2 and 3 above, and also by Butler, Dungan, Sanders, Barrett, and Vincent Taylor, together with a chapter by J. B. Tyson, "The Two-Source Hypothesis: A Critical Appraisal" (437–52). One should also mention Farmer's more recent book, *Jesus and the Gospel* (Philadelphia: Fortress, 1982), in which he applies his method to the gospel tradition and canon.

[5] C. H. Talbert and E. V. McKnight, "Can the Griesbach Hypothesis Be Falsified?" *JBL* 91 (1972) 338–68; the rejoinder by G. W. Buchanan, "Has the Griesbach Hypothesis Been Falsified?" *JBL* 93 (1972) 550–72; and especially Tuckett's monograph.

[6] Tuckett, *Griesbach Hypothesis*, 187.

[7] Farmer, *Synoptic Problem*, 279.

[8] Farmer, *Synoptic Problem*, 279–83. He uses Tatian's *Diatessaron* as an example of such a gospel. D. L. Dungan develops this last argument, while dissenting from the suggestion of a cultic purpose; see his article, "Reactionary Trends in the Gospel Producing Activity in the Early Church: Marcion, Tatian, Mark," in *L'Evangile selon Marc, Tradition et Rédaction* (ed. M. Sabbe; Leuven: Leuven University Press, 1988) 179–202, especially 201–202. Tuckett, *Griesbach Hypothesis*, 52–56, criticizes Farmer's position.

Synoptists. Farmer has studied the *literary* phenomena almost exclusively in trying to show that Mark could have used Matthew and Luke alternately. But the function of redaction criticism, as it is now practiced, is to explain an author's *theological* purpose, and, to my knowledge, Farmer has not done this adequately. Without such an understanding, the literary phenomena are in a theological vacuum. What is needed is to test the hypothesis by studying Mark from this point of view with as great sympathy as possible, while not neglecting redactional features that may or may not be theological or at least not obviously so.

The thought which prompted the present study is that each of the gospels should be looked at as a whole before a judgment can be made as to which way the setting of Mark can best be understood. Thus I propose to examine the shape and the purpose (or apparent effect) of each gospel, and in each case to study the Christology, the eschatology, the function of parables and miracles, and finally the possible setting of Mark with respect to Judaism, Hellenism, and ecclesiology.

Tuckett's study necessarily focused on literary problems, for these are the basis of Farmer's argument. Defenders of the GH will no doubt answer some of his points, but it does not seem necessary to review his work, although in places I mention some of the passages he has studied. Thus I shall say very little about the duplicate expressions or pleonasms of Mark, his use of the historic present, the order of pericopes, the conflated texts, and the minor agreements. I must, however, deal with the choice of materials and a few of the Mark–Q overlaps, and devote considerable attention to the eschatological passages.

The debate may have entered a new stage with the publication of David B. Peabody's *Mark as Composer*.[9] Peabody aims to develop a

---

9   D. B. Peabody, *Mark as Composer* (Macon, GA: Mercer University Press, 1987). In order to have some idea of how these researches might be used, I noted down the verses in Mark which Peabody concludes to have the highest probability of coming from the evangelist's hand (162–63), together with a supplementary list of other verses which he thinks of as having almost equal rank (165). These I have compared with corresponding passages in Matthew which are more or less parallel. When these parallel verses are studied as a whole, and not merely with respect to the phenomena Peabody finds to be unique to Mark, there are eleven places where the two evangelists have much the same verbal syntax, i.e., in using finite verbs, genitives absolute, participles in hypotaxis, etc. There are also fourteen verses in which the syntax is quite different, i.e., Mark uses a finite verb (usually an aorist), while Matthew resorts to hypotaxis. Another study of οἶκος/οἰκία and κατ'ἰδίαν/κατὰ μόνας did not seem clearly to support either the GH or the 2DH. It seems likely that until publication of analyses of the styles of Matthew and Luke, similar to that of Peabody,

method that "presupposes no particular solution to the Synoptic Problem" (xv). He believes that he has found the proper way to isolate redactional features in Mark by using three criteria, the compositional function of the features within the gospel, their distribution within the gospel, and the interlacing of redactional features within the same literary context, (21–22).

In the Foreword to this book, which is the first of a projected series, Farmer promises that similar studies of Matthew and Luke will appear (x). It will be interesting to see reviews of the monograph, which ought to prove a helpful tool in the study of Mark's composition; still more interesting, to learn what conclusions supporters of the GH will draw from the studies of all three Synoptics. In my opinion, something more than this type of literary investigation is needed, but that is not to diminish the value of Peabody's work.

The conclusions which will appear at the end of this monograph, such as they are, may not be more persuasive than other attempts to deal with the Synoptic problem. Some matters will remain problematical. Our sources for knowledge of the development of early Christianity are relatively sparse and open to more than one interpretation. What I hope to have done is to suggest a method for study of the problem which other students may be able to correct and refine.

Something should perhaps be said about Farmer's elaborate review of the debate in the 19th and 20th centuries. He maintains that defenders of the 2DH were influenced by theological positions which they held, "that 'extra-scientific' or 'nonscientific' factors exercised a deep influence in the development of a fundamentally misleading and false consensus."[10] This, he says, is not to say that there was a "conscious connection between the two document hypothesis and developmental and evolutionary social theories, but that the Marcan hypothesis exhibited features which commended itself to men who were disposed to place their trust in the capacity of science to foster the development of human progress."[11]

There is some justice in this criticism, particularly as regards 19th century German critics. It must be said, however, that the 2DH hypothesis is now defended by scholars who represent a wide variety of theological positions, so that his observations are not very relevant to the present

---

not much use can be made of this research in determining the priorities of the three gospels.

10   Farmer, *Synoptic Problem*, 190.
11   Farmer, *Synoptic Problem*, 179.

state of the debate. Farmer has confined himself to literary analysis. Yet there is always the possibility that some supporters of the GH may have been influenced, especially in the past, by their own theologies, for if the priority of Matthew can be demonstrated it can be helpful to one or more theological positions.

Nevertheless, Farmer has raised an important question of methodology. The present study assumes that it is proper to take theological development, or at least theological variety, into account in studying the Synoptic Problem. This is the approach followed in present-day redaction criticism. Of course one should not naïvely suppose that there are laws of development which operate in a straight line. The proper method should begin with the literary phenomena and go on to the theological issues disclosed. I began this study intending to keep an open mind, but the longer I worked the more I was convinced that the 2DH is far from obsolete, and is much more easily defensible than the GH. Examination of the shape of the three gospels and their theology seems to me to show that in most cases the comparisons confirm the judgment that Matthew and Luke are secondary to Mark, and that the Q material has a primitive theology of its own.

I wish to express my gratitude to Professors Charles H. Talbert and L. William Countryman, who read this monograph at various stages of its development, to Professor Adela Yarbro Collins and readers for the Monograph Series, who offered helpful criticisms, to Dean Judith Berling of the Graduate Theological Union, who arranged a grant to defray the cost of word processing, and to Bonnie J. Elliott who patiently prepared much of the typescript.

CHAPTER ONE

The Shape and Theology of Mark

The structure of Mark, which has been studied extensively in the last generation, is significantly different from the shape of Luke and, to a lesser extent, from that of Matthew. The first task is to discuss how Mark has organized his gospel and the theology that is disclosed thereby. Mark's redactorial work is often easily discernible. Sometimes this has theological implications; at other times it is simply a matter of the evangelist's stylistic habits. In either case, observation of his work is useful when compared with the other Synoptic gospels.

This chapter will concentrate on structure and provide an overview of Mark, and this will inevitably lead to questions about the gospel's theological meaning. Certain larger issues of structure and theology (e.g., the Reign of God and Christology) will, however, be considered more fully in other chapters.

The outstanding peculiarities of Mark's gospel are that it begins with the preaching of John the Baptizer and the baptism of Jesus and ends with the empty tomb, and that there are significant differences between 1:1–8:26 and the remaining part (approximately half) of the gospel, in which everything leads toward the Cross and its sequel.

The GH demands a new look at the shape of Mark and especially comparison with the structures of Matthew and Luke, for it assumes that the evangelist revises previous attempts to tell the story of Jesus, in order to produce a sharp and stark narrative, to which he gives the heading "The beginning of the Good News of Jesus Christ the Son of God"(1:1).

Thus it is supposed that Mark is not the first to write a gospel but yet composes what is often taken to be the prototypical gospel, in which Jesus' life is framed by the *incipit* and the words of the centurion, "Truly this man was Son of God"(15:39).

Clues to Structure

Besides the observation that the gospel has two principal parts, there are other significant clues to its structure: summary sections, both major and minor; the turning point of the gospel (8:27–9:1), transition sections, the three predictions of the Passion and other groups of three, and the anticipation of themes that are to be developed in a later part of the gospel. Thus there are short summaries in 1:32-34; 1:39; 4:33-34; 7:35-36; and 12:38a. The major summary in 3:7-12 must be significant. A brief but important passage occurs at 6:53-56, following a statement on the hardening of the minds of the disciples (6:52).

The verse just mentioned looks forward to a crucial dialogue in 8:14–21 on the subject of the loaves of bread, which in turn introduces the healing of the blind man of Bethsaida (8:22-26). This miracle, not found in the other gospels, serves as a transition to the Caesarea Philippi and Transfiguration scenes.

There are three major sections in which Jesus teaches his disciples, 4:1-34 (the Reign of God and parables); 9:30–10:45 (from Galilee to Jerusalem); and Chap. 13 (the coming of the Son of Man). The collection in Chap. 12 is presented as public teaching. It corresponds to a series of controversies in 2:1–3:6. 9:30–10:45 is important because its teachings link up with 8:27–9:1 and expose what it means to follow Jesus on the way of the Cross. The healing of Bartimaeus (10:46-52) is a transition pericope.

This brief survey, and the analysis of Matthew in Chap. 2, show that while Mark's structure roughly parallels that of Matthew, it is entirely different from the latter's pattern of narrative sections and discourses. It is a little more like the shape of Luke, in which there is a Central Section of teaching as Jesus leads his disciples to Jerusalem.

A Shorter Gospel

Problems begin immediately after the first verse. St. Augustine was not the last reader of the gospel to suppose that Mark was an abbreviator who did not need the well-known story of Jesus' birth and for whom it was his ministry and saving death that were essential. But, if so, why did he insert a verse from Malachi into a quotation from Isaiah and ascribe the whole to Isaiah? There are other differences in 1:2-13 which bear on Mark's Christology and must be discussed.

The beginning of Mark can be explained from the 2DH, but in itself it provides no insuperable difficulty for the GH. There are other examples of a gospel with no infancy narrative. The Fourth Gospel, after the Prologue, gives the testimony of John the Baptist. It has no interest in Jesus' conception and birth, and Philip calls him the son of Joseph from Nazareth (1:45). This is how anyone in Galilee might have spoken of Jesus, but in any case this was no problem for the evangelist; the important truth is that Jesus is the Logos.[1]

Another Christian writing that can be compared is Marcion's edition of Luke, which begins with Jesus' sudden appearance at the synagogue in Capharnaum. One theory is that Marcion already had access to a shorter form of Luke. Marcion's father is said to have been a bishop in Sinope; if so, he could have found such a book in that city.[2] Marcion was evidently a docetist, as John and Luke were not; without preliminaries Jesus began his ministry of revealing the "stranger" God. Mark, like the other evangelists, believed in Jesus' genuine humanity, and it would seem that he had no interest in the problem of docetism, whereas Luke and John were conscious of it.

The ministry begins when Jesus arrives in Galilee. His announcement, which together with 1:1 is the keynote of the gospel, is usually translated in some such way as this: "The time is fully come, and the

---

[1]   The thesis of Robert T. Fortna, *The Gospel of Signs* (Cambridge: Cambridge University Press, 1970) and his more recent study, *The Fourth Gospel and its Predecessor* (Philadelphia: Fortress, 1988), would suggest that the Signs Gospel is a very early example of a gospel without an infancy narrative; cf. Lamar Cope, "The Earliest Gospel was the Signs Gospel," in *Jesus, the Gospels, and the Church* (ed. E. P. Sanders; Macon, GA: Mercer University Press, 1987) 17–24. Some scholars would classify this gospel as an aretalogy, and one may compare the collection in Mark studied by Achtemeier; see note 9 below.

[2]   The tradition is in Epiphanius' *Panarion*; see John Knox, *Marcion and the New Testament* (Chicago: University of Chicago Press, 1942) 1–2. I still have questions about Knox's conclusions which I expressed in my review of this book, *ATR* 25 (1943) 228–33. Knox continued to hold that canonical Luke is quite late, for there is no evidence for its existence before A.D. 150. See his article, "Marcion's Gospel and the Synoptic Problem," in Sanders, *Jesus, the Gospels, and the Church*, 25–31. It is hard to explain why certain portions of canonical Luke are not found in Marcion's gospel. Not all of them are from material peculiar to Luke. They also include parallels to Mark–Matthew and to Matthew (Q), and it is curious that 19:29–46 is lacking. Knox's statement that "Marcan passages in Marcion's Luke could have been derived from Matthew" is more serious, and calls for further study.

Reign of God has drawn near; repent and believe in the Good News"(1:15).[3]

The First Part of the Galilean Ministry

Jesus apparently makes Capharnaum his headquarters after the calling of the first four disciples (1:16-20), and in 1:16–3:6, together with the summary section 3:7-12, his activity is on the west side of the lake near that town. The first miracle is in the synagogue, the exorcism of the man with the unclean spirit (1:21-28 = Luke 4:31-37; lacking in Matthew).

Here two points emerge. (1) Mark thinks of Jesus as teacher, but in the other gospels relatively more of Jesus' teaching is recorded. The miracle caused people in the synagogue to exclaim, "What is this? A new teaching with authority!" Mark pictures Jesus as teaching more through action than through words; in fact, the two activities go together. (2) The demon recognizes Jesus as the Holy One of God (1:24; cf. 1:34; 3:11, "the Son of God"); and the demons fight back (here and in 5:7-9). Thus they know a secret hidden from others. The Reign of God is not mentioned between 1:15 and 4:11 and one asks whether Mark regards Jesus' deeds of power as manifestations of the Kingdom. The saying in 3:23-25, in which Beelzebul or Satan has a kingdom that is coming to an end, may be evidence that God's Kingdom is waging war against the demonic realm, but Mark does not say this directly.

The theme of the secret of Jesus' nature (usually referred to as the "messianic secret") has emerged. The disciples evidently do not understand it, for when Jesus retires to the hill country to pray, they hunt him down, and he has to say that his purpose is to preach elsewhere.[4]

After the healing of the leper, which has some traits of a conflict with demons,[5] Jesus returns to Capharnaum and heals the paralytic (2:1-12). Into this miracle is inserted a controversy in which Jesus declares that the

---

[3] W. H. Kelber, *The Kingdom in Mark* (Philadelphia: Fortress, 1974) 7–12, notes the perfect πεπλήρωται and the use of ἐν τῷ εὐαγγελίῳ instead of εἰς τὸ εὐαγγέλιον, which one might expect after πιστεύετε. He therefore translates: "Believe on the basis of the Good News." Kelber takes this proclamation to mean that in Jesus' activity the Kingdom has arrived, and partly on this builds his case that the primary message of Mark is the Kingdom of God in the "new place" and "new time."

[4] T. J. Weeden, *Mark—Traditions in Conflict* (Philadelphia: Fortress, 1971) 26–32, understands this as the beginning of a continuing lack of perceptiveness on the part of the disciples. He holds that later this incomprehension turns into stubborn disobedience.

[5] ἐμβριμησάμενος, ἐξέβαλεν, 1:43. In v. 41 it is at least possible that ὀργισθείς (D etc.) is the correct reading.

Son of Man has authority on earth to forgive sins (2:10). This title appears only here and in 2:28 prior to Peter's confession; thus, early in this gospel, Mark suggests a mystery of the Son of Man, later to be explained. This is in sharp contrast to the way in which Matthew and Luke use the title.

The healing of the paralytic constitutes a transition, for it is the first pericope in an important collection of controversies (2:1–3:6). This section has been studied in detail by Joanna Dewey, who uses a method she calls rhetorical criticism (in distinction from redaction criticism and literary criticism in general), and concentrates on how Mark structured the passage as it stands. She concludes that the structure reveals a concentric and chiastic pattern which the evangelist has imposed upon the individual traditional elements. This pattern puts several themes into relationship, the nature of the conflict between Jesus and his opponents, healing and eating, life and death, and the nature of the role played by Jesus' disciples.[6]

If one looks at this section and its parallels from the point of view of the GH, it is evident that Mark could not have derived it from Matthew. Here he agrees with the order of Luke 5:17–6:11; the corresponding parts of Matthew are 9:1-17; 12:1-14. Likewise the content agrees more closely with Luke, though Mark is fuller. For example, "Levi" in Mark 2:14, Luke 5:27, "Matthew" in Matt 9:9; and in Matt 9:13; 12:5-6, 11 there are materials not found in the other gospels. If Mark had used Luke, he ignored Luke 5:39 and added a second Son of Man saying (Mark 2:27, "the sabbath was made for human beings, not human beings for the sabbath"). Here the 2DH appears to be the better solution.

The remaining pericopes in Chap. 2 consist of the call of the tax collector Levi (2:14), Jesus' eating with tax collectors and sinners which includes his saying that the healthy do not need a physician (2:15-17), the dialogue on fasting (2:18-22), and the controversy over plucking grain on the sabbath (2:23-28). The entire chapter is bound together by the theme of the contrast between the old and the new, which is highlighted by a saying in 2:19a and a double saying in 2:27-28. The fasts in question may have been voluntary, though Mark does not indicate this; in that case participation in them was a mark of behavior appropriate to religious

---

6 Joanna Dewey, *Markan Public Debate: Literary Technique, Concentric Structure and Theology in Mark 2:1–3:6* (SBLDS 48; Chico, CA: Scholars Press, 1980) especially 129, 181–97.

persons but not required by the law.[7] Jesus' answer is that fasting is out of place now, for the time is like a wedding party (2:19), but there is also an anticipation of Jesus' death (2:20). Reaping and threshing on the sabbath were of course prohibited by Torah, and Mark provides two sayings: human need overrides the Sabbath; Jesus as Son of Man is lord of the sabbath and therefore his decision is final (2:27-28).

The healing on the sabbath evokes another controversy in which Jesus is personally involved, and here he gives a different kind of answer which from the scribes' point of view would be irrelevant (3:4). The sayings that Mark has included have already shown that there is no way of reconciling the old and the new (2:21-22), and now deadly hostility has arisen (3:6). Here the Herodians appear alongside the Pharisees. Later Jesus is to warn his disciples against the leaven of Herod (8:15), and in 12:15 Herodians and Pharisees will again be coupled.

Mark's important summary section (3:7-12) provides a contrast to the opposition that has just developed. Crowds from all parts of Palestine as well as from Transjordan and the region of Tyre and Sidon press upon Jesus, asking for healing, so much so that he has the disciples arrange for a boat, which will be mentioned again in 4:1.

Thus ends the first phase of Jesus' Galilean ministry. The parts of Matthew that correspond roughly with this are 4:17–9:34, in other words Matthew's first "book," including the Sermon on the Mount, and the narrative portions of the second book. The comparable part of Luke runs from 4:16 through 6:11. The GH would explain the phenomena by saying that Mark uses Matt 4:18-22 (call of the first four disciples) but picks up Luke's order at 4:31, omitting some parts that are peculiar to Luke. If so, Mark has edited the material in 1:21-3:12 with characteristic touches of his own, e.g., in 1:44 and 3:6.

The Choice and Training of the Twelve

The selection of the Twelve (3:13-19) marks a further development in Mark's story, and much of the account through Chap. 6 has to do with the training of these special disciples through word and example.

Opposition is heightened in the Beelzebul controversy (3:22-30). The complicated literary relationships of this pericope are to be discussed later. The controversy is framed by 3:20-21, in which οἱ παρ' αὐτοῦ

---

7 D. Daube, "Responsibilities of Master and Disciples in the Gospels," *NTS* 19 (1972) 1–15, especially 4. 2:23–28 is discussed by Talbert ("Can the Griesbach Hypothesis Be Falsified?" *JBL* 81 [1972] 353–57.)

(presumably Jesus' family) came to seize him, for they said "he is beside himself," and 3:31-35, when Jesus' mother, brothers and sisters arrive, and Jesus declares who the true members of his family are. 3:20-21 is found only in Mark.[8] This prepares for the story of Jesus' visit to his home village (6:1-6), where the people in the synagogue reject him, but Jesus' saying includes the family also: "among his kin and in his house" (6:4).

The Parables Discourse

The apparent break between Jesus and his family is followed by the parables discourse (Mark 4:1-34). Perhaps Mark's thought is that Jesus will test out the Twelve to see if they will be more receptive.

Detailed differences between the three gospels in this discourse will be discussed later, but a few phenomena may be noted here. Mark 4:1-20 runs generally parallel to Matt 13:1–23 and Luke 8:4–15 and this section consists of three parts, the parable of the Sower, a few verses on the mystery of the Reign of God, and the explanation of the Sower. Matthew's form is sometimes more brief here, but he adds other material in 13:12, 14–15 and also in 13:16–17. The effect of the latter is to emphasize the contrast between outsiders, who do not understand, and the disciples who do, whereas Mark 4:13 implies that Jesus' companions are ignorant. In contrast, the section in Luke is smooth and brief.

The remainder of Mark's discourse (4:21-34) is significantly different from the corresponding parts of Matthew and Luke. Mark 4:21-25 is paralleled in Luke 8:16-18, while Matthew has some of these sayings in different contexts. Luke's group of parables ends at this point and he goes on to tell of the visit of Jesus' family (8:19-21). Mark alone has the parable of the Seed Growing Secretly, or the Patient Farmer (4:26-29), while the parable of the Weeds appears at this point in Matthew (13:24–30). The parable of the Mustard-seed follows in Mark 4:30–32 and Matt 13:31–32, and Matthew now includes the Leaven (13:33); Luke has the two in a different context.

Mark concludes the discourse in 4:33–34. Matthew contains a transition section somewhat similar to this, but he then adds one of his quota-

---

[8] Matthew places the visit of the family at a later point (12:46–50). Here we learn only that the family wishes to speak with Jesus, and 12:47 is textually insecure. Luke has the pericope in a different context and in brief form (8:19–21), but he also has a dialogue in 11:27–28 which makes a similar point.

tions with the characteristic formula (13:35), then gives an interpretation of the Weeds and follows it with other parables.

Miracles

Up to this point the structures of Mark and Matthew have been very different. To a lesser extent this is true also of Luke, but both Matthew and Luke have inserted forms of the great Sermon.

The shape of Mark 4:35–8:26 may have been determined partly by two catenae of miracles, collected prior to Mark, which Paul Achtemeier has identified.[9] In this case Mark has inserted other material in accordance with his theology with the result that the pattern has been modified.

Mark first tells of a series of miracles in 4:35–5:43, namely the storm at sea, the Gerasene demoniac, the raising of Jairus' daughter and the healing of the woman with the haemorrhage. Luke 8:22–56 has these in much the same context, after the Parables discourse, although with the visit of Jesus' family (8:19–21) intervening. These miracles are found in Matt 8:23–34; 9:18–26, with sections parallel to Mark 2:1–22 in between. The 2DH and the GH give different explanations of this phenomenon, which will be discussed in connection with Matthew's structure.

In this connection, Mark's topography may be of some importance. The evangelist had mentioned a boat in which Jesus sat as he spoke the first of his parables (4:1). It is now ready in the evening when he and his disciples cross the lake and a storm comes up (4:35-41).

Mark, more than the other evangelists, pays attention to geography. There are many topographical details in Chaps. 1–8, and the crossing of the lake at this point is an example. Since K. L. Schmidt's monograph, form critics have argued that the framework is artificial.[10]

---

[9]   P . J. Achtemeier, "Toward the Isolation of Pre-Markan Miracle Catenae," *JBL* 89 (1970) 265–91; "The Origin and Function of the Pre-Markan Miracle Catenae," *JBL* 91 (1972) 198–221. There are two catenae with parallel structure: (A) a sea miracle, 4:35–41; three healings, 5:1–20; 5:21–24, 35–43; 5:25–34, and a miraculous feeding (6:30–44); (B) a sea miracle, 6:45–52; three healings, 8:22–26; 7:25–30; 7:32–37; and a miraculous feeding, 8:1–10. Achtemeier finds that all of these are epiphanic and reflect a divine man Christology. His scheme assumes that Mark has transferred the healing of the blind man (8:22–26) to its present position to create another pattern. Kelber, *Kingdom in Mark*, discusses how Mark has constructed 4:35–6:44 as the interaction of the Kingdom with the Jews (48–57) and 6:53–8:26 as a section focusing on the Gentiles (57–65, 70).

[10]   K. L. Schmidt, *Der Rahmen der Geschichte Jesu* (Berlin: Trowitzsch, 1919).

Certainly Mark's story line is designed for a theological purpose. The most recent and thorough discussion of this is that of Elizabeth Struthers Malbon, who has combined two methods, Lévi-Strauss's schemata of mythical space and contemporary structural exegesis. In this way she has been able to show why Mark has modified Achtemeier's original explanation of the underlying catenae. Although the evangelist's purpose is theological throughout, his topography is lifelike and consistent, particularly when corresponding passages in Matthew and Luke are compared with it.[11]

The exorcism of 5:1–20 is obviously in pagan territory, and at the end Jesus departs from his usual practice of forbidding mention of his healings, for he tells the man who is restored to sanity to go to his own people and report to them how many things the Lord (the true God) has done for him. This is the only time when Jesus is in Gentile territory prior to 7:21. This is an example of how Mark anticipates a theme early in his narrative and later develops it. In the sequel Jesus will heal at least one Gentile and proclaim that the Temple is a house of prayer for all nations. At his death, a centurion (perhaps a pagan) will recognize him as a son of God.

Whether or not the first of Achtemeier's catenae lies behind this part of the gospel, this group of miracle stories has other definite theological

---

[11] Elizabeth Struthers Malbon, *Narrative Source and Mythic Meaning in Mark* (San Francisco: Harper & Row, 1986). "On the surface, the Markan topography is neither startling nor unimaginable, but as a narrative representation of the world it bears significance for the overall meaning of Mark. The patterns of movement of Jesus and the others within topographic space suggest Jesus' response to the world and the world's response to Jesus" (68). It appears that, according to Mark, Jesus sent the disciples in a boat *toward* Bethsaida (Mark 6:45) but they never arrived there, and Jesus brought them back safely to Gennesaret (6:53). They do not actually come to Bethsaida until much later (8:22; see note 9 above). Malbon's explanation (27–29) is that now Jesus engages in a controversy over the purity laws, has a ministry in the Tyre and Sidon region, heals the deaf-mute and feeds the Four Thousand. All of this emphasizes the blindness of the disciples. I do not agree with the theory of Kelber (*Kingdom in Mark*, 61) that the disciples reached Bethsaida about the time of the storm and that Dalmanutha was on the east side of the lake; cf. also Malbon, "The Jesus of Mark and the Sea of Galilee," *JBL* 103 (1984) 363–77, especially 370–73. She criticizes part of Kelber's discussion of the Achtemeier theory, but agrees with him that the symbol of the lake bridges the gulf between Jewish and Gentile Christians (373, n. 29). Kelber remarks that Mark seems to be spokesman for the Galilean Christians. "The gospel sponsors a Christianity of the north. . . Galilee in its broadest sense, including the Decapolis and the area of Tyre and Sidon, furnishes the setting in life for Mark the evangelist" (*Kingdom in Mark*, 130–31).

purposes. The stilling of the tempest shows Jesus' power over nature, and it corresponds to the wild storm in the mind of the demoniac. Jesus raises Jairus' daughter from apparent death (5:21–24, 35–43) and into this inserts the healing of the woman with the ailment that had made her ritually unclean (5:25–34; cf. the discussion of the clean and unclean in 7:1–23). Matthew tells of the two healings very briefly (9:18–26), Luke in rather more detail (8:40–56), but Mark's account is the most detailed of all. If he has been copying Matthew, he learns from that gospel the device of sandwiching an incident into parts of another, and applies it in other places (e.g., 3:20–35; 11:1, 12–14, 15–19, 20–25).

The Rejection of Jesus at Home

The next scene is Jesus' rejection (6:1-6a). Mark knows that Jesus is known as the Nazarene or Nazoraean, and Matthew that he lived in Nazareth, but both gospels here mention only Jesus' πατρίς, home village or homeland. Perhaps the word heightens the pathos or irony of the scene. We should particularly note Jesus' remark: "A prophet is not dishonored except in his own home town and *among his kin and in his own house*" (6:4). Crossan finds in this pericope a polemic against the family of Jesus which must have existed in Palestinian Christianity in the first century.[12] Matt 13:53–58 matches Mark's account in the main, with some exceptions. Jesus is not called the "builder," but the son of the builder; instead of "the son of Mary" we have the question "Is not his mother named Mary?" and most importantly, the words "and among his own kin" are lacking in 13:57. Matthew had also preserved the saying about Jesus' true family (12:50 = Mark 3:35).

Luke's account of the rejection in Nazareth makes no allusion to the family except for the question of the villagers, "Is not this Joseph's son?" (4:22). Otherwise he has no parallel to Mark 6:1–6a but he does include in a different context the blessing on Jesus' mother from a woman in the crowd and Jesus' rejoinder, "Rather, happy are they who hear the word of God and keep it" (Luke 11:27–28).

Further information about the family comes from other sources. Paul's letters are the earliest of these. He knows of James, who is the first of the brothers mentioned in Mark 6:3 (Matt 13:55). In general he speaks

---

12   *Gos. Thom.* combines this logion with the one in Luke 4:24: "There is no prophet acceptable in his own neighborhood, nor does a physician do healings among those who know him." This may well be the original form. If so, it is Mark who has added the criticism of Jesus' family; cf. J. D. Crossan, "Mark and the Relatives of Jesus," *NovT* 15 (1973) 81–113.

of him with respect, unless he is ironical when he remarks that James, Cephas and John were "regarded as pillars" (Gal 2:9), and he does not directly criticize James in Gal 2:11–12. It is Cephas whom he rebukes for ceasing to eat with Gentiles after "certain ones from James" came to Antioch, apparently claiming to act on James' authority. It must be this same James whom Paul mentions as a witness of the Resurrection (1 Cor 15:7). Finally, Paul considers that the brothers of the Lord and Cephas have the right to take their wives with them when they go on apostolic journeys (1 Cor 9:5).

Likewise James is a respected figure in the Book of Acts. He emerges in Chap. 15 as the leader of the Jerusalem church; his statement, delivered after Peter's appeal on behalf of the Gentiles, forms the basis of the decree of the conference (15:22–29); and Paul on his last journey to Jerusalem reports to James and the elders (21:18).

These records are probably the basis of the late tradition that James was the first bishop of Jerusalem (Eusebius *H.E.* iii. 11–12; iv. 22. 4) and the account of the appearance of the risen Lord to him in the Gospel according to the Hebrews (Jerome *de vir. inl.* 2). Another indication of the importance of Jesus' family in first century Palestine is the tradition that the grandsons of Jude, who farmed in Galilee, were brought before Domitian, and on their release and return governed the churches (Hegesippus in Eusebius *H.E.* iii. 20. 1–6).

These traditions, taken together, make it likely that the Lord's family had enough authority and influence so that there could be a struggle for power. We do not know, however, who made up the opposition to it; possibly those who considered themselves followers of the Twelve, more likely the Johannine community, for Jesus' brothers come under criticism in John 7:1–9. They wish him to go to Judaea to make a public display of his works, and the evangelist adds that they did not believe in him. His mother does not understand him entirely, but she is loyal (John 2:3–5), and she is with the beloved disciple, Mary of Clopas and Mary Magdalene at the Crucifixion (19:25); no blame attaches to her.

Matthew and Luke reflect almost none of this opposition. They honor Mary as the virgin mother of Jesus, and in Luke she is the one to whom the wondrous birth is announced, who visits Elizabeth, sings the *Magnificat*, ponders intelligently the remarkable events of Jesus' infancy and childhood (2:5, 19; cf. 2:34–35), and in Acts 1:14 she is associated with the Eleven after the Ascension.

It is Mark and John, then, who are least friendly to Jesus' family. Matthew and Luke appear to have softened the criticism. The alternative is that Mark sharpens it, and also especially portrays the Twelve in an unfavorable light.

Success and Failure of the Twelve

The Twelve are sent out on their mission, and in spite of their previously demonstrated weakness they are successful in exorcism and healing (6:6b–13). Mark is the only evangelist who says that they anointed with oil.[13]

Now Herod Antipas hears of Jesus' fame and makes the superstitious conjecture that he is John the Baptizer risen from the dead (6:14–16). The opinion of others, that Jesus is Elijah or one of the prophets, is to be echoed in 8:28. Mark goes on to tell of the martyrdom of the Baptizer in greater detail than does Matthew (Mark 6:17–29 = Matt 14:3–12). The apostles return and report to Jesus (6:30), and two great miracles follow.

The feeding of the Five Thousand (6:31–44) is remarkable in its greater detail, as compared with the parallels, e.g., the men are like sheep without a shepherd, and on the green grass they are like so many garden plots, assembled like a Jewish army in hundreds and fifties (6:39–40); and it is especially interesting that Jesus first taught them "many things" (6:34); Matt 14:14 mentions healings, while Luke 9:11 combines speaking of the Reign of God (a feature characteristic of Luke) with healing.

All three gospels present the event much as if it were a eucharist or a solemn meal—Jesus "looked up to heaven, blessed and broke;" the disciples distribute the food like deacons and gather up what remains.[14] Luke omits the miracle that follows and therefore the feeding immediately precedes Peter's confession that Jesus is "the Messiah of God" (Luke 9:20).

The multiplication of the loaves and the walking on the water (6:45–52) are the climax of the miracles presented in the first part of Mark's gospel. The former affirms Jesus' ability to feed his people; the latter proclaims his divinity and his presence with them when they face crisis ("I am," 6:50).

---

[13] Kelber (*Kingdom in Mark*, 53–55) sees 6:1–6a as the point at which Jesus, having broken with the family, sends the Twelve out to be his apostles, even though at the end the Twelve fail to apprehend the meaning of the Kingdom (145–47).

[14] So also in John 6:1–13 except that John does not record the breaking of the bread. Jesus, however, commands the disciples to collect the fragments left over.

The pericope begins with Jesus and the disciples crossing the lake to Bethsaida.[15] Matthew does not mention this place (14:22), but Luke does so in 9:10 with the result that the feeding miracle and presumably Peter's confession take place east of the Jordan; but Luke makes nothing of this topographical item. There are other differences between Mark and Matthew. Mark says that Jesus was about to pass by the disciples as he came near them (6:48). This is another indication of Jesus' divinity; God's ways and purposes are not those of mortals. After Jesus has reassured the disciples, Matthew adds the story of Peter's attempt to walk on the waters (14:28–31). The motive is the testing of Peter's faith, and the style is Matthaean (ὀλιγόπιστε, εἰς τί ἐδίστασας), but the pericope in Matthew ends with the disciples worshipping Jesus and proclaiming, "Truly you are God's Son." Mark, however, leaves the disciples in extreme astonishment, "for they did not understand about the loaves, but their minds were obtuse" (6:52).[16]

As Jesus' miracles have come to a climax, so has the stupidity of the disciples. In Mark's scheme this prepares for the discourse on the loaves (8:14–21). After the walking on the water, Jesus, now in the boat with his disciples, crosses to Gennesaret. The section 6:53–56 is an elaborate summary of Jesus' healings (cf. 1:45 and the major summary 3:7–12); and Mark alludes to previous parts of the narrative by using the words κραβάττοις (2:4, 11) and τοῦ κρασπέδου τοῦ ἱματίου αὐτοῦ (5:27; Matt 9:20). This concludes the section that began at 3:13.

The Recalcitrance of the Disciples

This high point of the disciples' failure is an important part of T. J. Weeden's argument. He regards the portrait of the disciples, rather than the messianic secret as such, as the hermeneutical key to Mark's construction, and holds that the evangelist intends to discredit the disciples

---

[15] We have already noted Achtemeier's conjecture that in the source this was preliminary to the story of the Blind Man (8:22–26), which Mark displaced (cf. also Kelber, *Kingdom in Mark*, 58).

[16] Quentin Quesnell, *The Mind of Mark* (Rome: Pontifical Biblical Institute, 1969) regards this verse as the key to the understanding of Mark's purpose. The "breads" were intended to evoke no fewer than seven "values and experiences that can be summed up as eucharistic" (257–58), and these involve the entire mystery, including the passion, death and future coming of the Lord, salvation for Jew and Gentile, and the union of believers in Christ. Quesnell finds special connection of the verse with 4:1–34; 7:1–23 and 8:14–21. His argument cannot be discussed here. The point that concerns us is that he has at any rate disclosed patterns in Mark that could not be derived from Matthew or Luke.

totally. There are three stages in the development, the unperceptiveness of the Twelve (1:16–8:20), their rebellion (8:27–14:9), and their final rejection of Jesus, which begins with Judas' betrayal in 14:10–11.[17]

Whether or not one accepts this thesis completely, his marshalling of the evidence makes it clear that, as compared with Mark, Matthew and Luke are far more gentle in their criticism of the disciples. In the pericope on the mystery of the Reign of God, Matthew inserts, after the quotation from Isaiah, the beatitude "But blessed are your eyes, for they see. . ." (13:16). Peter is congratulated for confessing Jesus as Messiah and is invested with authority (16:16–19). Even though Peter's faith is imperfect, he tries to walk on the water, and all the disciples hail Jesus as Son of God (14:28–33). They will sit on thrones judging the twelve tribes of Israel (Matt 19:28; cf. Luke 22:28–30). It is not James and John who ask for places of honor, but their foolish mother (Matt 20:20). These phenomena are not as striking in Luke, but they are present.[18]

In contrast, the discourse on the leaven in Mark 8:13–21, which is a key passage for Weeden and especially for Quesnell, leaves the disciples with complete lack of understanding, whereas in Matt 16:12 they finally get the point.[19]

If one approaches the problem on the basis of the GH, with Weeden's thesis in mind, much of current redaction criticism of Matthew and Luke is turned upside down. The effect is to strengthen many of Weeden's arguments and to say that Mark deliberately undermines Matthew and Luke and their tradition.

The "heresy" that Weeden uncovers is not a heresy in the later technical meaning of the term, for as yet the Church has no orthodoxy. It consists in a triumphalist view of Jesus. He is victorious, he reigns in glory, and it is the Resurrection not the Cross which discloses his true nature; he is a θεῖος ἀνήρ and he can bestow on his disciples the power to be θεῖοι ἄνδρες likewise.

Weeden's case proceeds from the widely accepted thesis of Dieter Georgi that the "superlative apostles" whom Paul had to combat in 2

---

17 Weeden, *Traditions in Conflict*, 26–51.
18 See comments on Weeden in note 4 above.
19 Much of Mark 8:13–21 is in Mark's style, but some of the peculiarities appear also in Matt 16:5–6. Matthew's style is, however, seen in 16:6, which reads προσέχετε (a verb which Matthew uses six times, Mark never). The verse also has "Sadducees" instead of "Herod." Matthew mentions this party eight times, Mark only once (12:18).

Corinthians were men who claimed to be larger than life, with supernatural powers of eloquence and miracle.[20]

It is an unquestionable fact that in 1:1–8:26 Jesus is portrayed generally as a successful worker of miracles—despite some opposition and much misunderstanding—and that from this point on the gospel is dominated by the suffering of the Son of Man and the way of the Cross.

We can also see that Mark is very reserved in his use of the title Messiah. It appears in 1:1, and although at Caesarea Philippi the disciples are told to be silent (8:30), Peter cannot be totally wrong in uttering the universal Christian acclamation.[21] Yet Mark is concerned that Jesus' unique messiahship should be properly understood, and therefore he is identified as the suffering Son of Man (8:31). Likewise, Jesus is able to acknowledge to the high priest that he is Messiah the Son of the Blessed, whereupon he speaks of himself as the Son of Man (14:62). The scribes say that Messiah is son of David, but, if Jesus is that at all, he is much more (12:35–37). Jesus warns against false messiahs.[22] Otherwise the word appears in the mockery of the chief priests (15:32) and in the singular verse 9:41, which looks like an intrusion from Matt 10:42, although it is textually secure.

The weakest part of Weeden's argument is that the glorious portrayal of Jesus in most of Chaps. 1–8 and the success of the disciples in 6:12–13 represent the divine man theology of the disciples which is set up only to be knocked down. The stories in Chaps. 1–8 seem to be told with great delight. And are the disciples always disloyal? At any rate, they follow him to Jericho and Jerusalem, even though they continue to misunderstand and run away at the time of the Crucifixion. And where could Mark have derived his tradition except from such people as the Twelve and their followers?[23]

---

[20] D. Georgi, *The Opponents of Paul in Second Corinthians* (Philadelphia: Fortress, 1986).

[21] E. Haenchen, "Die Komposition im Mk VIII:27–IX:1" *NovT* 6 (1963) 81–109.

[22] Weeden, *Traditions in Conflict*, 77–78, regards this as important. Luke omits Mark 13:21–24.

[23] For an example of criticism, see R. C. Tannehill, "The Disciples in Mark," *JR* 57 (1977) 386–405. J. D. Kingsbury, *Conflict in Mark: Jesus, Authorities, Disciples* (Minneapolis: Fortress, 1989) 8–14, 89–117, does not mention Weeden, but generally agrees with his scheme of rebellion that ends in apostasy, except in two respects. The disciples follow, except at the end; and because Mark 14:25 (cf. 16:7) looks forward to the reunion in Galilee, they will finally be reconciled to Jesus. Thus, in relation to the disciples, this is not a tragedy, but a divine comedy.

Certainly Mark, more than any other evangelist, preserved for the Church the insight of Paul that the Resurrection can be understood only in the light of the foolishness of God, the Cross through which humankind is saved. The tendency to forget this and to concentrate on Jesus' power can be observed in the traditions preserved by Papias, the apocryphal infancy gospels, and elsewhere. The only question is whether Mark affirms the glory of Jesus' deeds in Galilee and balances this with the message of the suffering Son of Man.

Mark may have been very subtle, but ordinary Christians who first heard or read his gospel would have taken the stories at face value as representing part of Mark's own message; they would have marvelled at the stupidity of the disciples, but they would remember the miraculous feedings and the walking on the water whenever they celebrated the Lord's Supper and when they were in danger of persecution and "the wind was contrary to them."

Achtemeier, of course, is concerned to deal with Mark's redaction of an underlying source. He believes that Mark has inserted Jesus' teaching into the source (6:1–13, 34b) and that he plays down the eucharistic character of the feeding miracle, for he wishes to show that it is the Last Supper which is the true model of the Eucharist.[24] The question remains, would the readers of the gospel perceive these subtle variations?

A Ministry among Gentiles

The next major section runs from 7:1 through 8:21 with a transition passage, 8:22–26. The effect of this is to continue the exhibition of Jesus' divine power and the story of his ministry among Gentiles, first foreshadowed in 5:1–20, and finally to contrast Jesus' success here with the obstinate stupidity of the disciples (8:14–21). The parallel to this last pericope in Matt 16:5–12 is in sharp contrast; once the disciples have been taught, they understand.

This will include Achtemeier's second catena of miracles. In the latter part of this section, commentators have noticed another pattern consisting of doublets, as follows:

6:30–44	the Five Thousand	8:1–9	the Four Thousand
6:45	to Bethsaida	8:10	to Dalmanutha
6:47–51	Sign of Walking on Water	8:11–12	no sign will be given

---

[24] Achtemeier, "Origin and Function," 218–21.

| 6:52–53 | lack of understanding | 8:14–21 | lack of understanding |
| 6:53 | crossing of lake | 8:13 | crossing of lake[25] |

One may ask whether Mark has derived this pattern from Matthew. If he did, the walking on water in Matt 14:23–27 is matched by reference to the sign of Jonah (16:1–2a,4). In Matt 14:33 the disciples recognize Jesus as Son of God, while in 16:5–12 they understand Jesus' explanation of the loaves. The difficulty remains, however, that even in Matthew the disciples are perplexed and have to be taught. The pattern, such as it is, is clearer in Mark than in Matthew.

The controversy in 7:1–23 over cleanliness and the Korban vow marks a high point in the Jewish leaders' opposition to Jesus. This will be discussed further in connection with the position of the three gospels regarding Torah. It would almost seem that Jesus is in danger and has to leave Jewish territory for a time, for he departs for the region of Tyre (7:24).[26] Here Jesus would like to be incognito, but this is impossible; crowds from Tyre and Sidon had come to him at an earlier time (3:8). He now heals the daughter of the Syrophoenician woman (7:25–30). The point of the story is not the exorcism but the persistent faith of a Gentile, expressed with delightful wit.

Jesus now returns to the Sea of Galilee through the territory of the Decapolis, where he heals the deaf mute (7:32–37). This is a perfect example of a healing miracle in which physical means are used, and Jesus' Aramaic word *ephphatha* is reported. This must be an independent unit of tradition, for Mark can hardly have built it up out of Matt 9:32–33; 12:22 or Luke 11:14. Jesus is evidently still in a pagan region on the east side of the lake; Matthew at this point (15:29) simply has Jesus returning to the lake.

---

[25] Cf. S. E. Johnson, *A Commentary on the Gospel according to St. Mark* (London: Black, 1977) 136. The second group of passages is part of Luke's "great omission." The theory that his MS of Mark had a lacuna at this point is probably mistaken. He at least knew of the crossing to Bethsaida in Mark 6:45 because he mentions Bethsaida at 9:10. His motive was probably twofold, to delete Mark 8:1–9 (or Matt 15:32–39) as unnecessary, and to avoid criticism of the disciples. Omission of Mark 7:1–23 or Matt 15:1–20 is easier to understand because Luke had legal materials that he preferred. He also had a story of the healing of a Gentile and so did not need the narrative of the Canaanite woman (Matt 15:21–28) or the Syrophoenician (Mark 7:25–30).

[26] The alternative is that the pattern is similar to that one finds in Luke-Acts: "Since you judge yourselves unworthy of eternal life, we are turning to the Gentiles" (Acts 13:46; cf. 28:25–28).

The feeding of the Four Thousand (8:1–9) seems to occur in the same neighborhood and is a counterpart to the previous miracle; now Gentiles are fed. When Jesus now comes to the west it is to the otherwise unknown place Dalmanutha (8:10); at this point Matthew has the more understandable Magadan (15:39).

The Pharisees demand a sign; Jesus refuses this absolutely, and he and his disciples again depart to "the other side" (8:11–13). This introduces the dialogue occasioned by the failure of the disciples to bring bread aboard (8:14–21). No more important sign could have been given than the two miracles of the loaves, yet the disciples still do not understand. We have already remarked on the symbolism of Mark's redaction; the disciples are blind (8:18), and now the blind man of Bethsaida is given sight (8:22–26). The miracle is found only in Mark.

The evangelist may think of Bethsaida as the fishing village on the lake or as the larger Bethsaida Julias. In any case, this is still east of the Jordan and possibly in predominantly Gentile territory. Certainly Caesarea Philippi, in the next scene, is pagan[27] and the high mountain of the Transfiguration can be thought of as Hermon.

The blind man is healed in two stages. Afterward the disciples discern Jesus' nature, at first partially when he reveals himself as Son of Man, and then more clearly in the Transfiguration.[28]

The symbolism does not seem to work out perfectly, because even after the experience on the mountain the spiritual vision of the disciples is still imperfect; as contrasted with the sight of the man of Bethsaida. Perhaps the point is that on the mountain the full meaning of Jesus' nature was disclosed; it was only that Peter and the others refused to understand what they had seen.

Conclusions on 4:35–8:26

However artificial Mark's geography may be in 4:35–8:26 and later parts of the gospel, it is generally more lifelike and consistent than in the corresponding parts of Matthew and Luke. The structure of the miracles in 4:35–5:43 is coherent. Mark apparently has more than one theological purpose: to exhibit Jesus' divine power, to show this as Good News in action, healing and exorcising; and to indicate that the gospel will also come to pagans. The function of the miracles in Matt 8:1–9:35 could be

27   J. Murphy–O'Connor, *The Holy Land* (Oxford: Oxford University Press, 1980) 136.
28   Cf. Johnson, *St. Mark*, 144–45.

similar, but the primary purpose of this collection, which includes other miracles, is to serve as a model for the twelve disciples (9:36–10:1). This does not come out as clearly in Mark's form of the mission of the Twelve (6:7–13).

Mark's purpose, as seen in 4:35–5:43, continues down through 8:26. The principal difference between Matthew and Mark is that the latter evangelist portrays the Twelve as failing to understand Jesus' nature in spite of his mighty works, particularly in the multiplication of bread and the walking on the water.

Finally, one should consider Achtemeier's theory. Either Matthew has disrupted a catena of miracles or the catena is the construction of Mark, not of his source.

Caesarea Philippi

The dialogue is introduced by Jesus' question, "Who do people say that I am?" and the answers given recall earlier opinions (6:14–16). In answer to a further question, Peter says simply, "You are the Messiah," and Jesus forbids the disciples to speak about him (8:29–30). Here Luke is in agreement, though the form of the answer is "the Messiah of God" (Luke 9:20–21). But in Matt 16:20 the command is to tell no one that Jesus is the Messiah, and this comes after Peter's fuller confession "Messiah the Son of the living God" and Jesus' congratulation to Peter (16:16–19). Here it must be observed that Mark and Luke do not have these verses and that Matthew is the only evangelist to use the word ἐκκλησία.

The GH should say that Luke has made the omission and that in this he is followed by Mark. But in that case Mark has then turned back to Matthew and has rewritten Matt 16:22–23 (Mark 8:32–33), then in 8:34–9:1 has done further rewriting, mostly following Luke 9:23–27. This means that both Luke and Mark omit the prediction that when the Son of Man comes "he will recompense everyone in accordance with his deeds" (Matt 16:27b)[29] and that Mark changes the statement that the Son of Man will be seen coming in his kingdom to a promise that the disciples will see the kingdom of God (Mark adds "with power"; Matt 16:28 = Luke 9:27). Thus the two evangelists would have had to reject the idea that the Son of Man has a kingdom. This makes Mark and Luke radical revisionists, for they also ignore the special dignity which according to Matthew is given to Peter, although Luke says that Peter was the first to see the risen Lord (24:34) and he is the principal spokesman of the community in

---

[29] This appears to be Matthaean redaction. Note the καὶ τότε. ἀποδίδωμι is used by Matthew fourteen times, by Mark only once (12:17).

the early chapters of Acts. The 2DH appears to be a more satisfactory solution of the phenomena.

The Transfiguration

The blind man of Bethsaida was healed in two stages. The confession of Peter, as representative of the disciples, indicated some sight, but the vision was badly impaired, and in his discourse Jesus attempted to improve it. The story of the Transfiguration (9:2–8) implies a clearer sight. This contains several OT motifs, e.g., Elijah and Moses, the cloud on Sinai, and the booths of the Jewish festival, but the essence of it in Mark seems to be the foreshadowing of Jesus' future glory as Son of Man. This vision, and the voice from heaven, corresponding to the announcement at Jesus' baptism, ought to correspond to the second stage in the healing of the blind man, who then saw clearly, but the discourse as Jesus and the disciples descend from the mountain (9:9–13) shows that the healing of the disciples is at best partial. They had an open vision but could not understand how the Son of Man could rise from the dead. The significance of Elijah is that he has returned in John the Baptist and has been put to death, just as Jesus will die.

After the descent, Jesus heals the epileptic boy.[30] Mark's story (9:14–29) does not say whether the boy and his father are Jews or Gentiles, but the mention of scribes in 9:14 suggests a Jewish milieu, and it is not surprising that later tradition identified Tabor as the place of the Transfiguration. Yet, after this, when Jesus and his disciples go through Galilee it is secretly (9:30, a note that is not found in Matthew).

On the Way to Jerusalem

There is no longer any public ministry in Galilee, and all of Jesus' teaching in this region is given to the disciples in private (9:31–50). 9:31–10:52 is one of the principal collections of teaching in the gospel. The main themes, discipleship and the way of the Cross, resume Jesus' admonitions at Caesarea Philippi. Beginning with 10:1, the group is on its way to Jerusalem.

The corresponding parts of Matthew (17:23–20:34) contain nearly all the elements in the Marcan passages, but are much fuller and in fact mis-

---

[30] It is alleged that here the stories in Matthew and Luke are smoother than the one in Mark. Raymond E. Brown in his article, "The *Gospel of Peter* and Canonical Gospel Priority," *NTS* 33 (1987) 321–43, points out the weakness of an argument from smoothness (330–31).

cellaneous. One who follows the GH would say that Mark omits the dialogue on the Temple tax (Matt 17:24–27), which comes between the second Passion prediction and the dispute over rank; the parable of the Lost Sheep (18:10–14) and all the other material in Matt 18, including the parable of the Unforgiving Slave; and the parable of the Laborers in the Vineyard (20:1–16), which appears in Matthew after the divorce section. Mark, then, would have added the pericope of the Strange Exorcist (Mark 9:37–40) from Luke 9:49–50, and also Mark 9:41.

One can argue that elsewhere Mark deals with forgiveness and searching for the lost. Otherwise his motive for the omissions would have to be that he removed from Matthew all materials that did not suit his main purpose, the instruction of disciples who are to follow the way of the Cross. Mark's attitude to Torah will be discussed later. Here it can be said that a desire to avoid discussions of law would not account for omission of the Temple tax pericope and the section on church discipline (Matt 18:15–18), for Mark includes the discussion of divorce.

Mark, then, has a structure that is not seen clearly in the corresponding parts of Matthew. Each of the Passion predictions introduces teachings whose general theme is the attitude of disciples. Following the second Passion prediction (9:30–31) is a group of three pericopes on the general theme of "little ones."

The first of these is in two parts: the disciples' dispute over rank and Jesus' answer, the first must be last and slave of all (9:33–35) and a saying on the accepting of little children (9:36–37). Mark presents this as given in private after the company has returned to Capharnaum, and Jesus asks what the disciples had discussed "on the road" (cf. 8:27); the road will lead to Jerusalem and the Cross.

In Matthew there is no dispute among the disciples, only a question that they ask (18:1), while Luke knows of a contention (9:46). On the GH, Mark has had to skip back and forth between Matthew and Luke, adopting "Capharnaum" from Matt 17:24 and then turning to Luke. But Matthew makes the theme of children a teaching on humility, inserts a saying (18:3) paralleled in Mark 10:15, and the saying on receiving children (18:5 = Mark 9:37) comes in awkwardly.[31] The situation is just as bad in Luke 9:46–48, for the saying in verse 47 does not fit with the rest of the pericope. Mark has obviously put three separate ideas together: only

---

[31] Mark 9:37a and especially 10:14–15 show that there is a saying on children that existed in various forms; others occur in *Gos. Thom.* 21, 22, 33, 46b. It is probable that Mark did not derive the sayings from Matthew.

the servant of all can be first; to accept children is to accept Jesus; and to accept Jesus is to accept God. This last part of the logion (Mark 9:37b = Luke 9:48b) is a floating saying. In Matt 10:40 (= Luke 10:16; cf. John 20:21) it is used to express the apostolic principle: the authority of the apostles comes from Jesus, that of Jesus from God. Of the three gospels, Mark is the least awkward at this point, and it is easier to suppose that Matthew and Luke have edited Mark rather than the reverse.

The second pericope (Mark 9:38–40 = Luke 9:49–50) is the little incident of the Outsider Exorcist. Luke's form of this preserves only the essentials, while Mark is more wordy; "in your/my name" and "he does not follow us" appear twice. The strange saying about the cup of water given "because you are of Christ" (9:41–42; cf. Matt 10:42) comes at the end and seems to have been attracted here because of the words "in my name." There is every reason for Luke to have omitted it, and it is difficult to know why Mark would have added it to Luke. In Luke this pericope concludes a major section of that gospel. The story, I believe, refers to "little ones"because the disciples despise him; but he is on Jesus' side because he is fighting against the demonic kingdom and therefore a potential disciple; a stumbling block should not be put in his way.

The third group of sayings begins with scandals to "one of these little ones," i.e., actions which cause them to commit sin or possibly to lose faith (9:42), but in the next verses (45, 47–48) the scandal is something in the disciple's personality which leads him into sin. There follow sayings on salt (9:49–50), evidently here because of verbal linkage: children–little ones–scandals–fire–salt. In Matthew the only links are scandals–little ones; there is no clear linkage in Luke. Salt appears in Matthew and Luke in quite different contexts.

The phenomena in Mark 9:33–50 can best be accounted for if Mark is using source material, perhaps oral, in which various sayings are strung together. It would be curious if Mark had taken bits and pieces out of the other gospels to make up such a chain.

Luke's Central Section (9:51–18:14) takes the place of Mark 9:41–10:12 or Matt 18:8–19:12.

A second group of three pericopes follows the sayings in Mark 9:42–50. The first of these has an editorial introduction which marks a stage in Jesus' journey; he now moves east of the Jordan (10:1). The section on little children enshrines Jesus' word "Truly I tell you, whoever does not receive the Kingdom of God like a child will not enter it" (10:15) and reinforces the teaching of 9:37. This, and the pericope of the Rich Man (10:17–

22) and the accompanying dialogue (10:23–31) definitely concern discipleship.

What, then, is the function of the divorce pericope (10:2–11)? It may be simply a quasi-legal piece which is to serve as guidance for future church leaders. I have, however, suggested that there is a pattern resembling a *Haustafel* in Chaps. 9–10: "little ones," 9:33–42; married people (10:1–12); children (10:13–16); rich men (10:17–27); and church leaders (10:28–30, 35–45).[32]

If this is a possible pattern, we may have three patterns here, one geographical, one based on the Passion predictions, and a series, which although it is not in *Haustafel* form, reminds one of passages in Colossians, Ephesians, the Pastorals, and 1 Peter. Mark's structure does not have a single outline. Lohmeyer noted groups of threes and elaborate interconnections; I have said, "in fact the gospel can be likened to an oriental rug in which many patterns cross one another. They are not made up with mathematical exactitude but developed spontaneously as the author writes."[33]

There may be still another reason why Mark placed 10:1–12 at this point. The prohibition of divorce, as compared with Matt 19:3–9; 5:31–32, is much more strict, and even Matthew's less stringent rule evoked the objection: "If it is this way with husband and wife"—no release from a bad marriage—"it is better not to marry at all!" And Matthew, who of all the evangelists is most sensitive to Judaism, transmits a saying of those who have made themselves eunuchs (celibates) because of the Kingdom of the heavens (19:10–12).

---

[32] Johnson, *St. Mark*, 168–69. Professor Countryman remarks to me that in first century culture children and wives were considered almost to be kinds of property. The whole *Haustafel* could therefore be focused on property, for even rank in the Kingdom might be thought of as a possession. The Roman law of the *paterfamilias* certainly treated wives and children as chattels. The question here, however, concerns Jewish law. The rule ascribed to Jesus is much more strict than the law of the Mishnah. Judith Romney Wegner, *Chattel or Property? The Status of Women in the Mishnah* (Oxford: Oxford University Press, 1988) shows that Mishnaic law is more complicated. A woman is treated as property *only* when her biological function belongs to a specified man *and* the case poses a threat to his control of that function (vi, 168). In matters of private law, women are persons and virtually equivalent to men (6). Thus an adult daughter, a divorcee or a widow (except for a widow subject to the levirate law) has legal control of her own biological function (169). It is not known how much of this tradition goes back to the time of Jesus, but it is probable that the Pharisees treated women generally as persons.

[33] Johnson, *St. Mark*, 23.

Mark's divorce pericope, which rules out both a second marriage and polygamy, may therefore look in an ascetic direction. This seems especially possible if one considers that doing the will of God is more important than family ties (3:34–35) and that there are those who have left their families, even their children, for the sake of Jesus and the Reign of God (10:29–30). Luke 18:29 adds "wife" to those who are left behind, and in 14:20 one of the excuses offered for not coming to the banquet is "I have married a wife." It may or may not be significant that Philip's daughters, who were prophets, were unmarried (Acts 21:9). Of all the evangelists, Luke has the greatest love for poverty and the most distrust of riches. The Gospel of Thomas contains several sayings in favor of celibacy and a virginal life. Although this may be partly due to ascetic tendencies in northeast Syrian Christianity, other sayings in Thomas are independent of the Synoptic tradition, and at least some of Thomas' sayings on celibacy may be very primitive.[34]

Mark's editorial introduction to the third Passion prediction (10:33–34) is dramatic and solemn. Jesus and the disciples are "on the road" going up to Jerusalem. Jesus walks in front of them, and they are filled with awe. This third prediction is more detailed and seems to be developed out of the two previous ones. It is followed by just one teaching dialogue (10:35–45) which begins with the request of James and John, resumes the theme of 9:33–35, and is extremely powerful. The death of Jesus, announced just before this, means that he gives his life as a means of freeing the many (10:45).

If Mark borrowed this section from Matthew, he placed the blame directly on the two disciples instead of on their foolish mother (Matt 20:20); but in Matthew's account Jesus speaks directly to the two brothers as though the request had come from them (20:22). It is therefore likely that it is Matthew who has edited Mark here.

Conclusions on 8:27–10:45

The healing of the blind man of Bethsaida, found only in Mark, prepared the way for the Caesarea Philippi pericope, which is the turning point of the gospel. The scheme of three, which is characteristic of Mark, is a progressive opening of eyes, and in the Transfiguration scene the nature and destiny of Jesus are fully revealed. The three Passion predictions announce Jesus' work; he will be handed over, suffer, and rise again. Although the disciples do not fully understand, they follow him

---

[34] See e.g., J. D. Crossan, *Four Other Gospels* (Minneapolis: Winston, 1985) 33–37.

physically toward Jerusalem and are struck with awe (10:32). On the road they are taught the way of the Cross, the renunciation of possessions, family, rank, and even life. This central teaching section concludes with the interpretation of Jesus' work: he comes to serve and to give his life as a ransom (a means of freeing) the many (10:45).

Matthew contains most of this material, with the exception of the amazement (holy fear?) of the disciples (10:32), but the dramatic force of the narrative is somewhat weakened by the inclusion of other pericopes which, however, provide practical teaching adapted to the Church's needs and interest. If one follows the GH, Mark has revised Matthew so as to bring the scandal of the Cross into higher relief.

This section in Mark should be seen against the background of the first half of the gospel. Mark has balanced Jesus' miracles of power with the suffering of the Son of Man, in the light of which the nature and work of Jesus must be understood. The contrast is somewhat obscured in Matthew and Luke.

Bartimaeus

The last pericope before Jesus approaches Jerusalem (10:46–52), like the healing of the man of Bethsaida, is a transition section. It is located just at the point when he is leaving Jericho. Instead of Matthew's less colorful account of the two blind men (20:29–34; cf. 9:27–31), Jesus gives the single beggar a name, Bartimaeus, i.e. son of Timaeus, and tells the story in more detail. If Mark has developed the story out of Matthew and Luke, he has done it skillfully. Matthew does indeed say that the two men who had been healed followed Jesus (20:34), but Mark adds that they followed him *on the road*. Thus Bartimaeus has become a disciple. While he was blind he had hailed Jesus as son of David; now, like the man of Bethsaida, he sees clearly.[35]

Jesus in Jerusalem

The public ministry in Jerusalem is narrated in Matt 21–23 and Mark 11–12. (In Luke, even the eschatological discourse of 21:5–36 is spoken in the Temple; see 21:37–38). If Mark has been using one of the other

---

[35] The possible literary relations between this pericope and Matt 9:27–31; 20:29–34 can be interpreted in more than one way. Signs of Mark's style are clearly evident, but Matt 20:29 has the genitive absolute as Mark does, and 20:32 has also Jesus' question "What do you want me to do for you?" In Matt 9:27, παράγοντι ἐκεῖθεν appears to be Matthaean style, and καὶ appears in 9:28. Mark's εὐθὺς (10:52) is paralleled by εὐθέως in Matt 20: 34 .

gospels, it is Matthew; parallels to Luke are usually not as close, though at one point the plot against Jesus is mentioned (Luke 19:47–48; Mark 11:18–19).

In Matt 21:12–17, Jesus "cleanses" the Temple as soon as he enters Jerusalem, and this is followed by healings and the acclamation of children, after which he goes to Bethany to spend the night. The next morning he curses the fig tree, which withers immediately. The disciples marvel at this, whereupon Jesus speaks of faith and believing prayer (21:18–22).

In Mark, however, Jesus enters the Temple enclosure, looks around at everything, and then departs for Bethany (11:11). As Kelber remarks, this looking, is "critical or even judgmental." It is on the next morning that he curses the fig tree and then goes into Jerusalem and cleanses the Temple. The authorities plot against Jesus, and he goes out of the city in the evening (11:12–19). The action in the Temple is not so much a cleansing as a judgment on the Temple and its cult.[36] This observation fits with the fact that Jesus has first cursed the fig tree (cf. Luke 13:6–9, the prediction in Mark 13:2, and the charge made later that Jesus threatened to destroy the Temple, 14:53).

On the next morning, as Jesus and his company return to the city, Peter notices that the fig tree has now withered, and Jesus speaks of faith and prayer (Mark 11:20–25) more fully than in the parallel, Matt 21:21–22. The incident of the fig tree is more than a judgment on the Temple; it is also a promise. As Sharyn Dowd has argued, the sayings here attributed to Jesus are an instruction for the Marcan community, which has superseded the Temple as a house of prayer for all nations. Its prayer of petition is effective when it is uttered in faith and by a church whose members forgive one another freely (11:25). Here the plural verbs are significant.[37]

Supporters of the GH might assume that Mark has expanded the account in Matt 21:12–22 and has borrowed the substance of 11:25 from

---

[36] Kelber, *Kingdom in Mark*, 98–102. Kelber understands the vessels carried through the Temple to be sacred vessels, not ordinary objects brought through the Court of the Gentiles as a short-cut. I question this, because the latter explanation fits well with Jesus' word, "a house of prayer for all nations," i.e., the enclosure where Gentiles worship is sacred also.

[37] Sharyn E. Dowd, *Prayer, Power, and the Problem of Suffering: Mark 11:22–25 in the Context of Markan Theology* (Atlanta: Scholars Press, 1988), especially 53–55, 65–66. Kelber offers a theological explanation (*Kingdom in Mark*, 103), but does not discuss 11:25.

Matt 6:14. The strongest argument for this is the phrase "your Father who is in the heavens." Except for this peculiarity, it is easier to suppose that Matthew has abbreviated Mark. His form of the story ignores Mark's more lifelike detail that the tree withered overnight, and he fails to understand that the community, with its prayer of faith and mutual forgiveness, is the new house of prayer. Dowd's interpretation preserves the integrity of the pericope in Mark. The evangelist Mark perhaps derived the sayings in 11:22–25 from oral tradition, in which such sayings are strung together (cf. Mark 9:49–50).[38]

The story line in Mark 11:27–12:37a is essentially the same as in Matt 21:23–22:45, but two of Matthew's parables, the Two Sons (21:28–32) and the Great Supper (22:1–14), have no parallel in Mark. The GH could easily explain these as omissions, but it seems more likely that Matthew has inserted them. The first is on the obvious theme of saying and doing; the second predicts the first Jewish War, which is apparently interpreted in Mark 13:14–21 as one of the signs of the end.

Mark has portrayed Jesus as rejecting the established authorities by his action in the Temple, interpreting it to his disciples by the symbolic miracle of the Fig Tree, and he now refuses to tell the chief priests, scribes and elders by what authority he has acted.

The parable of the Wicked Tenants (12:1–12) completes the condemnation. In its present form this is not a typical parable but an allegory in which Mark evidently understands the "beloved son" to be Jesus; the slaves who were sent, prophets; the tenants the Jewish people; and those "others" who will later tend the vineyard, the Christians. In Mark the owner sends three slaves, then many others, and finally the son; Matthew speaks only of two groups of slaves who were sent. It has been argued that Luke is nearest the original, for he mentions only three successive slaves and then the son.[39]

But *Gos. Thom.* 65 must be the most primitive form of the parable that we have, for here the rule of three is preserved completely: there are two slaves and the son is the third. Furthermore, Thomas' parable is not alle-

---

[38] 11:26 is omitted by B ℵ and some other important MSS and versions, and the verse probably does not belong to Mark's text (cf. Dowd, *Prayer, Power, and the Problem of Suffering*, 40, 55). There is also evidence for omitting "who is in the heavens" in 11:25. Dowd, 42, notes that "your Father who is in the heavens" is a formula which is pre–Matthaean.

[39] J. A. T. Robinson, "The Parable of the Wicked Husbandmen: a Test of Synoptic Relationships," *NTS* 11 (1975) 443–61. He remarks, incidentally, that in this parable Matthew uses Mark (461).

gorical. There is also the curious fact that the saying respecting the cornerstone, which all three evangelists have, follows immediately as logion 66. Thus the two are connected in very early tradition but with no explanation given.

When we consider relations between the three gospels, the GH might lead one to argue that Luke has used Matthew, but in that case he has introduced the rule of three though not perfectly, for the son makes a fourth. Mark would then have copied Luke rather than Matthew, except that he adds 12:5 to indicate that many prophets were sent. It would not be like him to emphasize the "fruits" as Matthew does (Matt 21:41, 43). All three evangelists use the quotation from Ps 118 to point up the allegory. On the other hand, the 2DH would explain all the phenomena equally well.

It is curious that in Mark 12:12 and Luke 20:19, the authorities understand that the parable was spoken against them, while Matthew does not say so. Luke reduces the idea of secrecy in Jesus' teaching even more than Matthew (e.g., in Luke 8:10), but Mark 12:12 seems to contradict 4:11–12. The allegory of the parable is, however, transparent, and Jesus has just rejected the authorities (11:27–33).

The parable is not explicitly connected with the Reign of God; it is essentially Christological, with an eschatological warning. Mark may, however, have thought of the vineyard as representing the Kingdom, for the ultimate source of the imagery is Isa 5:1–7.

The total effect of Mark 11:27–12:37 is to highlight the growing hostility which leads to the Passion. This is relieved only by the dialogue with the scribe in which Jesus gives the summary of the law (12:32–34). It is particularly to be noted that in the last dialogue (12:35–37a) Jesus declares that the Messiah is David's Lord, not his son. The tension in Chap. 12 of Mark can be observed in Matt 21:28–22:46 also. It is made even more extreme in Matthew's next chapter.[40]

Chapter 23 of Matthew and its parallel, Luke 11:37–54, present special problems. One of these, obviously, is the question of Q. In this part of the study we are, however, concerned with Mark's possible use of Matthew. The parallels are sparse, essentially Mark 12:38b–39 = Matt 23:6–7 and 12:40 = Matt 23:14, which is textually insecure, since its most important witnesses are the Ferrar group and the OL.

---

[40] For the structure of 12:13–37a, see D. Daube, "Four Types of Question," *JTS* n.s. 2 (1951) 45–48.

On the basis of the GH, one would be forced to say that Mark is following Luke 20:45–47. He would then have borrowed the story of the Widow's Mite (12:41–44) from Luke 21:1–4. In the case of this pericope, why would Mark have taken Luke's neatly composed account and made it into his more wordy, almost colloquial story?

Chapter 13 and Parallels

As Farmer says, Chap. 13 of Mark is powerful and climactic and prepares for the Passion narrative.[41] If Matthew is Mark's source, he follows Matt 24:1–36 in general but with some curious changes. Tuckett has offered a very complete answer to Farmer's thesis regarding Matt 24 and its parallels, and McKnight has discussed Matt 24:37–39 = Luke 17:26–30 in detail. Here I review only some outstanding points.[42]

The GH requires that Mark has inserted in 13:9–13a materials on persecution of the disciples from Matt 10:17–22a. But it is natural for Mark to place these sayings here, for the disciples were not warned of persecution when they were first sent out (6:7b–13), and the command to take up the cross (8:34) accords with Mark's method of anticipating a teaching that will be given later.

It is the apparent omissions that are most striking. Mark would have to substitute 13:33–37 for Matt 24:42–51 (= Luke 12:41–46) with a free composition that has distant parallels to Matt 25:13–15; 24:42. He also omits Matt 24:26–28 (= Luke 17:24, 37b); 24:37–41 (= Luke 17:26–27, 34–35); and of course the eschatological parables of Matt 25. The result is a tighter discourse which makes the coming of the Son of Man appear more imminent.

The difficulties for the GH are not so much in these omissions as in the Matthaean details which are lacking in Mark's parallels to Matt 24. There are touches characteristic of Matthew which Mark omits or changes, e.g., 24:3 τῆς σῆς παρουσίας καὶ συντελείας τοῦ αἰῶνος (cf. παρουσία, 24:27, 37, 39). Matt 24:14 teaches that this gospel of *the Kingdom* must be proclaimed to the whole inhabited world before the end can come. The change from 24:15, "standing in a holy place," to Mark 13:14, "standing where he should not," could be accounted for by the GH if

---

41 W. R. Farmer, *The Synoptic Problem: A Critical Analysis* (New York: Macmillan, 1964) 279.

42 C. M. Tuckett, *The Revival of the Griesbach Hypothesis: An Analysis and Appraisal* (Cambridge: Cambridge University Press, 1983) 167–85; C. H. Talbert and E. V. McKnight, "Can the Griesbach Hypothesis be Falsified?" 364–68. Cf. notes 4 and 5 in the Introduction above.

Mark wished to make the prediction more vague, but the 2DH serves equally well; the same is true respecting "nor on a sabbath" (24:20). But the strangest phenomena are in Matt 24:30–31 (= Mark 13:20–21): the sign of the Son of Man in the sky, the mourning of the tribes and the sound of the great trumpet. I can think of no good reason why Mark should omit these, whereas they fit with Matthew's tendency to add allusions to the OT.

In all three gospels the same flat statement is found almost verbatim, "Truly I tell you, this generation will not pass away until all these things occur" (Matt 24:34 = Mark 13:30 = Luke 21:32), but the end seems to be delayed when Matthew says that the gospel must first be preached to all nations (24:14). Thus the end must be very late in Matthew's "generation." The conclusion of the discourse in Luke (21:34–36) warns against debauchery and worldly cares and bids the readers to be watchful in every season. Luke expresses this gracefully but in general terms. Mark's conclusion of the eschatological discourse is more dramatic.

There are actually two parables. The brief example of the fig tree (13:28–29) and its appended sayings (13:30–32) are found in Matthew and partially in Luke. The parable of the Absentee Master (13:33–37) is the conclusion. Its literary relationships are tantalizing, for it begins with language similar to the parable of the Talents (Matt 25:13–15), but its substance is similar to the conclusion of a Lucan parable (12:38) and the parable of the Thief at Night (Luke 12:39–40).[43] The night is divided into four watches (the Roman reckoning), not three, as in Luke.

The function of the parable is significant. It relates not to the Reign of God, as in Chap. 4, or to Jesus' death, as in the parable of the Wicked Tenants, but to the need for watchfulness, presumably for the coming of the Son of Man. This shows that Mark has chosen his parables to relate to the three primary interests of his gospel.

By its relative simplicity and this parable at the end, Mark 13 preserves a much higher eschatological tension than do the other gospels. Certainly in the period after the composition of Matthew and Luke (late 1st or early 2nd century) there was an equally vivid hope, as one can see from the Book of Revelation and Papias. But the GH presumes that Mark wishes to revive this when it is fading, and other attempts to do so that are known to us such as the Shepherd of Hermas and 2 Peter, have a different character.

---

[43] Tuckett, *Griesbach Hypothesis*, 183–85.

The Passion Narrative

The Passion Narratives in Mark and Matthew have the same general outline; that of Luke is significantly different. Several passages in Matthew have no parallel in Mark. The latter's account is relatively simple and straightforward, so much so that since Dibelius, and until recent years, the prevailing opinion was that it constituted a single source except for a few passages introduced by Mark, such as the anointing in Bethany (14:3–9) and the Gethsemane scene (14:32–42)[44] More recent study, however, sees the narrative as Mark's thorough redaction of fragmentary traditions in which OT passages, especially from the Psalms (e.g., 22, 69) and Isa 52:13–53:12, exercised a creative force. Johannes Schreiber's theory, that there were two strands of tradition in the Crucifixion story itself, has been influential. The older of these represents a primitive Jewish–Christian apologetic which alludes to Ps 22:18 and Isa 53:12.[45] The other is Hellenistic, reflects apocalyptic interests, and employs secrecy motifs, e.g., from 1 Cor 2:8 and Phil 2:6–11. This is related to Hellenistic epiphany stories in the θεῖος ἀνήρ tradition. The two strands are woven into a single story.[46]

Thus far, if Schreiber's theory is correct, it will apply whether the GH or the 2DH theory is accepted. But Matthew and Luke contain several items not found in Mark.[47] Most of these are miraculous and could be considered examples of the theology of glory. Note especially Matt 27:54, in which the centurion and the guards are struck with fear by the earthquake and *all* say, "Truly this was a Son of God." If one is to sup-

---

[44] Cf., e.g., M. Dibelius, *The Message of Jesus Christ* (New York: Scribners, 1939) 30–34; F. C. Grant, *The Gospels: Their Origin and Growth* (New York: Harper, 1957) 79.

[45] T. J. Weeden, "The Cross as Power in Weakness," in *The Passion in Mark* (ed. W. H. Kelber; Philadelphia: Fortress, 1976), 117. It is recognized that, although Mark's Passion Narrative is composite, the main outlines of the stories of the trial and crucifixion were remembered and form the basis of the narrative.

[46] J. Schreiber, *Theologie des Vertrauens* (Hamburg: Porsche, 1967) 24–40, 66–82. Matthew has parallels to all the traditions listed by Schreiber, which are as follows: (1) Older tradition: 15:20b, 22, 24, 27; (2) Hellenistic: 15:25–26, 29a, 32c, 33–34a, 37. In Luke there are only three exceptions. Luke does not have a parallel to the "led him away" or "led him out" of Matt 27:31b = Mark 15:20b (cf. Isa 53:7, "led like a lamb to the slaughter"), the wagging of heads of Matt 27:50 = Mark 15:29a (cf. Ps 22:7), and the loud voice of Matt 27:50 = Mark 15:37. The first item is not significant, because Luke uses the Suffering Servant theme elsewhere.

[47] Matt 27:19, dream of Pilate's wife; 27:43 (cf. Ps 22:9); 27:51b–53, earthquake and appearance of the dead saints; Luke 23:34, "Father, forgive them;" 23:39b–43, the penitent bandit and Jesus' response; 23:45, the eclipse; 23:46b (cf. Ps 31:8).

pose that Mark wished to discredit miraculous elements or at least to tell a more sober story, why did he retain the darkness over the land and the loud cry (Mark 15:37, 39) if the latter is the shout of a hero?

Attempts to go behind Mark's Passion Narrative (or that of Matthew) are necessarily conjectural. The same is true of Dominic Crossan's theory that a source imbedded in the *Gospel of Peter* (= GP) 1:1–2; 3:5b–6:22 lies behind Mark. He uses a method he has applied to the *Gospel of Thomas* to argue the independence of this source of GP.[48] Proceeding on the basis of the 2DH, he holds that Mark used this source, but the GP as it stands is derived also from the other Synoptics. The reason for mentioning this here is that if one follows the GH as well as Crossan's theory a different scenario would have to be worked out; in that case, Mark redacts Matthew rather than the GP source. In any case, Mark's account places greater emphasis on the faith of the centurion. It is when he hears Jesus' last cry and observes how he died that he exclaims,"Truly this man was a son of God" (15:39). Matthew, as we have seen, speaks of "the centurion and those with him," and it is the earthquake and the other portents which evoke the exclamation (Matt 27:51–54).

So much for attempts to find sources and complicated redactions behind Mark's Passion Narrative. There are a few elements that make difficulties for the GH. I select two. (1) σαβαχθανί in Jesus' cry from the Cross (Ps 22:1) is apparently Aramaic and appears in both Matt 27:46 and Mark 15:34, but Matthew has Ηλί (Hebrew) for Mark's ἐλωΐ (Aramaic). (2) All three gospels mention Simon of Cyrene (Matt 27:32; Mark 15:21; Luke 23:26), but Mark speaks of him as the father of Alexander and Rufus in a way suggesting that his readers would know of these men. If this is not a genuine reminiscence, it is a sophisticated use of novelistic techniques.

The Empty Tomb

Mark contains no story of the appearance of the risen Lord. It is not that the Resurrection is not important to Mark—the three Passion predictions indicate otherwise—but this is not the end of the Good News, for the climax will be the coming of the Son of Man, which was prefigured in

---

[48] J. D. Crossan, *Four Other Gospels*, 137–48. Cf. A. R. Bellinzoni, "Extra Canonical Literature and the Synoptic Problem," in Sanders, *Jesus, the Gospels, and the Church*, 3–15. This article is suggestive, but evidence from this literature has to be handled with care; see the criticisms of R. E. Brown, "The *Gospel of Peter*," 321–43.

the Transfiguration and announced in 13:26 and 14:62, though Galilee is not mentioned in those passages.

In all three Synoptics the women are the first to hear the message of the Resurrection. In Mark, the announcement comes from a young man in a white garment,[49] who says, "Go tell the disciples and Peter, he goes before you into Galilee; there you will see him, as he told you"' (16:7). The women, however, are afraid, and tell no one (16:8).

In Matt 28:1–10, however, Mary Magdalene and "the other Mary" find the tomb empty, and an angel whose appearance is dazzling instructs them to send the disciples to Galilee, where they will see the risen Lord; then Jesus himself meets them with the same message.[50] The situation is quite different in Luke 24:1–11. Here the women are Mary Magdalene, Joanna, Mary of James and the other women from Galilee (23:49; 8:2–3), and they meet two men in shining clothing. These men do not say that the apostles should go to Galilee. When the women report the Resurrection to the Eleven they are not believed. Luke goes on to tell of Jesus' appearance on the road to Emmaus and to the Eleven in Jerusalem, and finally the Ascension.

Conclusion

The evidence given above tends to show that Mark is prior to Matthew and Luke and that the 2DH is to be preferred to the GH. This evidence consists of literary phenomena and also the theology of Mark as it is observed through redaction criticism. It will be supplemented in later chapters.

Mark could *theoretically* have derived the structure of his gospel from Matthew and Luke, except that Chaps. 8–9 of Matthew raise problems to be mentioned in the two next chapters. Mark's gospel, however, has a distinctive shape which does not easily emerge from the other gospels,

The story through Mark 8:26 leads up to the confession of Peter at Caesarea Philippi, and the second half of the gospel is dominated by the Passion predictions and the way of the Cross. Mark's transition sections

---

49 John Knox, "A Note on Mark 14:51–52," *The Joy of Study* (ed. S. E. Johnson; New York: Macmillan, 1951) 27–30, argued that the incident in the garden is an anticipation of the story of the Empty Tomb; cf. also H. N. Waetjen, "The Ending of Mark and the Gospel's Shift in Eschatology," *Journal of the Swedish Theological Institute* 4 (1965), 114–31.

50 Talbert discusses Mark 16:1–8 and parallels, concluding that Matt 28:1–8 is secondary (cf. Talbert and McKnight, "Can the Griesbach Hypothesis be Falsified?" 339–44).

are also distinctive. 3:7–12 could have been made up of bits and pieces from the other gospels, but it is more likely that Luke 6:17–19 is a rewriting of it. The story of the blind man of Bethsaida links artistically to the preceding discourse on the loaves and begins a pattern of blindness and sight unique to Mark. It is also, like the companion miracle of the deaf mute (7:31–37), a classic example of the miracle tale form.

Mark's topography, with its crossings of the lake and incursions into Gentile territory, may be artificial and designed for a theological purpose, but it is generally consistent and shows that the evangelist has some knowledge, however he may have derived it, of the geography of Galilee.

Other details throughout the gospel also speak in favor of the 2DH. Matthew's account of the confession at Caesarea Philippi is surely secondary to that of Mark. The structure of 9:33–10:52 is not easily borrowed from Matthew, and this is particularly so in 9:33–50, where, if Mark is not independent he would have had to take small pieces from Matthew and Luke. The mother of the sons of Zebedee (Matt 20:20; cf. Mark 10:35) is a secondary touch. Matthew seems to have rewritten Mark's account of the cleansing of the Temple and the cursing of the fig tree. Other scholars have sufficiently discussed the eschatological discourse (Mark 13 and parallels) and the resurrection stories. Finally, it seems more probable that Matthew has added miraculous elements to the Passion Narrative than that Mark has simply omitted them.

Thanks to redaction criticism, the main traits of Mark's theology are well known. It is not that the evangelist denies the value of Jesus' miracles, but that he puts this aspect of Christology into perspective; Jesus' greater glory is that he gives his life for others, and he is not thought of as the Davidic Messiah. Through the geography Mark shows that the mission to Gentiles is inevitable. The 2DH explains these phenomena satisfactorily. Mark's gospel is not a radical revision of the theological positions of Matthew and Luke; it is they who have made the changes, and Chapter 7 will give further arguments for this.

CHAPTER TWO

The Shape and Theology of Matthew

The Specific Nature of Matthew's Gospel

The purpose of this chapter is to show that, although Mark and Matthew share a vast amount of material in common, the purpose and method of the two evangelists are in many ways quite different. The hypothesis that Matthew has expanded Mark's story and adapted it to his specific purposes seems more probable than that Mark has made a radical revision of the other gospel. There is a prevalent opinion that Mark and John are the most kerygmatic gospels, i.e., they exemplify most sharply the purposes of a gospel as it is expressed in John 20:31, "These things are written that you may believe that Jesus is the Christ, the Son of God, and that believing you may have life in [or by] his name."

If Matthew is the earliest of the three Synoptics, it is indeed a gospel, but it is more than that. From one point of view, it is a sacred history connected explicitly with the OT. It begins with a royal genealogy of Jesus, tracing his descent from David and Abraham. This, together with the account of Jesus' conception, the annunciation to Joseph, and the Lord's birth, states one of the principal themes of the gospel; Jesus is the promised Messiah, son of David and also Son of God. He is Immanuel, God with us, and his very name, Jesus or Joshua, indicates that he will save God's people from their sins.

In the first two chapters, as in later parts of the gospel, Matthew uses four quotations from the OT (1:23; 2:6, 15, 18) and one allusion to a text or texts (2:23), all prefaced by a formula peculiar to this evangelist, which are designed to show that the events of Jesus' birth and childhood are fulfillments of prophecy. He also indicates, by use of typology, that Joseph and the holy family recapitulate the sojourn of the patriarch Joseph in Egypt, the Exodus and the entrance of Joshua ('Ιησοῦς in the

LXX) into the Promised Land. There are also probable echoes of Balaam's prophecy of the star, the gold and frankincense of Isa 60:6, the Nazirite vow made by Manoah and his wife (Judg 13:4, 7), and perhaps other passages.

Matthew has thus written a gospel cast in the form of a sacred history. Although it does not claim to be Scripture, the genealogy, which is reminiscent of OT lists, particularly in the P traditions, together with other features just noted, suggests that it is a supplement to the sacred books which uses materials of Scripture somewhat as various books of the Kethubim do in the third part of the Hebrew canon.[1]

The Overall Structure

A second important characteristic of Matthew is its coherent structure designed for catechetical purposes. This gospel serves as a manual both for leaders and teachers and for the faithful. In some places Jesus teaches the Twelve directly, in other places the "crowds" who symbolize all who are willing to listen to him.[2] All of the gospels have a teaching function, but Matthew exhibits this to a higher degree. The "scribe made disciple to the Kingdom of the heavens like a householder who brings out of his storehouse things new and old" (Matt 13:52) has been called a self-portrait of the evangelist.

One analysis of Matthew that has been persuasive was proposed by B. W. Bacon. He held that the gospel essentially consists of a narrative introduction, the birth and childhood of Jesus (Chaps. 1-2), five narrative sections, each leading to a discourse which is marked at the end by an

---

[1] Cf. Donn F. Morgan, *Between Text and Community* (Minneapolis: Augsburg Fortress, 1990) 91–96. Morgan discusses the process by which the Kethubim interpreted the Torah and the Prophets and ultimately became part of the Hebrew canon. Matthew and other NT documents depend on the Torah and the Prophets in an analogous way. But the Jesus tradition was a decisive new factor, and as a result the gospels correspond, more or less, to Torah; and the epistles and other NT writings, to the Former and Latter Prophets. Morgan is interested in the process by which authoritative writings become a canon, and the principal theme of his book is that this process is a continual interaction of texts with the needs and purposes of the community. My interest here is merely to show that it was natural for Matthew to write a gospel that consciously is linked to Scripture and that the existence of the Kethubim made this a natural thing to do.

[2] Paul S. Minear, "The Disciples and the Crowds in the Gospel of Matthew," *ATR*, Supplemental Series, No. 3 (March 1974), 28-44. For a study of Matthew as a catechetical manual, see R. Thysman, *Communauté et directives éthiques; la catéchèse de Matthieu* (Gembloux: J. Duculot, 1974).

easily recognized colophon (7:28; 11:1; 13:53; 19:1; 26:1-2) and at the end the Passion and Resurrection narratives.[3] Jack Dean Kingsbury is not impressed by this scheme, and holds that the gospel has three principal parts 1:1–4:16; 4:17–16:20; 16:21–28:20.[4]

The First Book

The five narrative sections inevitably include teaching, but the stories in them move the action along. Thus the first of these, which Bacon calls Discipleship, tells of John's baptism, the baptism and temptation of Jesus, his announcement of the Kingdom (4:17), the calling of the first disciples (4:18–22), and a summary section telling of Jesus' teaching and a great crowd that follows him from all parts of Syria and Palestine (4:23-25).

The Sermon on the Mount (Chaps. 5-7) follows immediately. Formally, it is addressed to Jesus' disciples, who must have been more than four in number and who symbolize the Church's leadership; but the context has the "crowds" in mind. This is an indication that Matthew is not interested in strict chronology and can assume that the readers already know something of the story.

As Bornkamm has shown, this discourse is carefully constructed and has two related themes, the Kingdom and its righteousness.[5] While the Good News is proclaimed to the "poor" ("in spirit"), there is equal emphasis on the moral qualities necessary for receiving the Kingdom. The discourse concludes with the parable of the Two Houses and the first colophon (7:28-29). The crowds are astonished by Jesus' teaching, "for he was teaching them as one having authority, and not as the scribes."

---

[3] B. W. Bacon, *Studies in Matthew* (New York: Henry Holt, 1930). Krister Stendahl, among others, adopts the basic idea (see his commentary in *PCB*, 770). Both he and I are uncertain whether Chap. 23 should be considered part of the fifth discourse (Chaps. 24–25); cf. *IB* 7, 248, 528.

[4] J. D. Kingsbury, *Matthew: Structure, Christology, Kingdom* (Philadelphia: Fortress, 1975) 1–25. Kingsbury's criticisms have some force, and he is certainly right in seeing 4:16–17 as marking an important division because 4:12–16 discloses one of Matthew's themes, that, as also in Mark, Galilee is the great land of revelation. The evangelist's quotation of Isa 9:1–2, introduced by one of his characteristic formulae, is eloquent and impressive. In this study I preserve Bacon's suggestion because in any case it is a second pattern which crosses the one that Kingsbury has identified.

[5] G. Bornkamm, "Der Aufbau der Bergpredigt," *NTS* 24 (1978) 419–32.

The Kingdom of the Heavens

Matthew's usual phrase is "the Kingdom of the heavens." Occasionally the text reads"Kingdom of God" (12:28; 19:24; 21:31, 43); this is probably due to the evangelist's sources.

In Matthew, John the Baptist is the first to announce the Kingdom (3:2), and Jesus does so only later (4:17). In Matt 3:11 and Luke 3:16, John also predicts the future wrath. The Coming One will baptize with the Holy Spirit *and fire.*

Matthew usually speaks of the Kingdom as a future event; later we shall note exceptions. The Kingdom is sometimes expressed through the myth of the Messianic Banquet (8:11–12; 22:1-14), and it is connected with the final judgment. As the Davidic Messiah, Jesus is the herald and perhaps the bringer of the Kingdom, but Matthew is unique in teaching that the Son of Man has a kingdom which embraces heaven and earth and is distinguished from the Kingdom of the Father (13:41-43). Peter is promised the keys of the Kingdom of the heavens (16:18).

Evidently Matthew has woven together various strands of traditions, and there are traces of the Jewish concept that in one sense God's Reign is and always has been a reality. The clause in the Lord's Prayer,"may your will be done, as in heaven so on earth" (6:10b) appears only in Matthew. The Matthaean phrase "Kingdom of the heavens" points toward this. It is only a question of when God's rule will be universally established and acknowledged. All three gospels are interested in the conditions for entering the Kingdom, but this is especially prominent in Matthew.

The Twelve and Jesus' Pattern for Them

The next section, Apostleship, consists of a narrative (8:1–9:35) and a discourse (9:36–10:42), with a colophon at 11:1. The exorcisms and healings and one other miracle, the stilling of the storm, are designed, as Bacon says, to set forth the"signs of an apostle" (2 Cor 12:12) which the disciples will be expected to perform in the future.[6] With these are interspersed the calling of Matthew with its saying on eating with tax collectors and sinners (9:9–13), the controversy over fasting (9:14–17), and the radical demands made on disciples (8:18–22).[7] This explains the differ-

---

[6] Bacon, *Studies in Matthew,* 187.

[7] The order matches that of Mark (and Luke) in 8:1–17; 9:1–17, but not elsewhere; cf. C. M. Tuckett, *The Revival of the Griesbach Hypothesis: An Analysis and Appraisal* (Cambridge: Cambridge University Press, 1983) 26–31, 35–36.

ences between the order in Matthew 8–9 and the parallels in Mark and Luke.

This artistic combination of themes leads to the discourse itself, in which Jesus selects the Twelve, sends them out and yet forbids them to go into pagan and Samaritan places. They will not have finished visiting the towns of Israel before the Son of Man comes. Jesus also predicts persecutions and teaches the necessity of confessing Christ. This fits the situation of the later Church, and, while Matthew has the leaders primarily in mind, some of the admonitions would apply to all Christians (e.g., 10:32–33)

The Old and the New

The third major section (narrative, 11:2–12:50; discourse, 13:1–52; colophon, 13:53) might be called the Hiding of the Revelation or the Old and the New. It begins with a section on John the Baptist in which the contrast between the two ages is mentioned (11:12–13) and concludes with the parable of the scribe who brings out things *new and old*. Actually, the principal accent in the narrative portion is revelation, for Jesus is proclaimed as the Servant of the Lord (12:15–16). The story of Jesus' ministry is developed further to exhibit controversy and rejection; note the woes on the Galilean cities (11:20–24) and the Beelzebul controversy (12:22–32). This last pericope, which is to be discussed later, was anticipated in 9:34.

The discourse is devoted entirely to parables of the Kingdom of the heavens,[8] and their interpretation. It falls into two parts. In 13:1-35 the crowds are present, and the remainder is spoken to the disciples in the house. The Sower and its interpretation, the Weeds, Mustard-seed, and Leaven are heard by the crowds, and this part of the chapter concludes with a formula citation (13:35) which speaks of parables as things hidden.

---

[8] In Mark and Luke, the Sower is not called a parable of the Kingdom, but the context, in which Jesus speaks of the secret of the Kingdom, shows that the evangelists think of it as belonging to the group of Kingdom parables. Whereas Mark and Luke speak of the harvest in ascending order, thirtyfold, sixtyfold and hundredfold, Matthew reverses this order. The GH would presuppose that Luke and Mark make the change. But the hundredfold climax fits better with the other seed parables, the Mustard-seed and Leaven. If Matthew is responsible for the different order, it must be to suggest that some of those in whom the seed is sown bring forth fewer good works.

There is also a very full formula citation of Isa 6:9-10 in 13:14–15. The discussion in 13:11–17 makes the point that the secret of the Kingdom has been given to "you" (evidently both the disciples and the crowds, as receptive hearers) while it is hidden from those outside: "Blessed are your eyes, for they see."[9]

If Matthew is consistent in his method of redaction, he postpones the explanation of the Weeds because its message is primarily for leaders in the Church.[10] It is they who are tempted to weed the field of "scandals and those who are lawless" with the result that they will destroy the wheat also. The Son of Man will send his angels to do the purging of his kingdom, a realm distinct from the future Kingdom of his Father (13:37–43). The parable of the Seine (13:47-50) makes a similar point. Both parables are presented as allegories.

The brilliant twin parables of the Hid Treasure and the Costly Pearl (13:44–46) might seem appropriate for any Christian to hear, but they have a special application to the intimate disciples who have chosen to follow Jesus wherever he goes, for they describe men who sold all their possessions (cf. Matt 19:16–29 and parallels). The collection of parables is rounded off by the picture of the Scribe (13:52).

Caesarea Philippi and the Church

The fourth major section consists of narrative, as always with much teaching included (13:56–17:27), a discourse (Chap. 18), with the colophon at 19:1. The high point of the narrative is Peter's confession at Caesarea Philippi (16:13–28), and this lays the foundation for the later Church. This pericope will be discussed in detail later.

Perhaps it is significant that the narrative portion begins with Jesus' rejection in his home village, and what Jesus says (13:57) implies that he has not been accepted even by his own family. This had been suggested by the last item in the previous narrative section (12:46-50); those who do God's will are Jesus' brother and sister and mother.

Herod the tetrarch now hears about Jesus and supposes that he is John the Baptist risen from the dead; then follows an account of John's martyrdom which is reported to Jesus (14:1–12).

---

9 It is true that after the parable of the Sower, the disciples approach Jesus (προσελθόντες, v. 10, a characteristic of Matthew's style), but unless Matthew is careless in his redaction, this is quite different in Mark 4:10–13.

10 J. D. Kingsbury, *The Parables of Jesus in Matthew 13* (Richmond: John Knox Press, 1969) 22–91.

The story of the Feeding of the Five Thousand in a deserted place comes next (14:13–21). This is the most astounding of the miracles thus far, and at this point it is important to notice how Matthew treats the revelation of Jesus' nature to the disciples, because in Mark their lack of understanding is continually brought out. In the birth story and elsewhere Matthew had already taught that Jesus is Son of God and Messiah. This is understood by readers of the gospel but was not necessarily imparted to the disciples.

They had, however, been taught that it is not enough to prophesy and cast out demons in Jesus' name (7:21–23). After the storm at sea they had asked, "What sort of man is this" (8:27). Some of them had heard that the bridegroom would be taken away (9:15); the Twelve had been told that the Son of Man would come before they had gone through all the cities of Israel (10:23); that acceptance by God depends upon confessing Jesus openly (10:32–33); and finally that the one who received Jesus received the One who sent him (10:40).

All of this *assumes* a revelation of Jesus' nature rather than making a direct proclamation. In 11:4–6, Jesus tells the disciples of John the Baptist about the miracles that have occurred, and this is apparently in the presence of the crowds (11:7). Then in 11:25–30 Jesus reveals his unique sonship and calls on his hearers to accept his easy yoke, but Matthew says nothing about the audience. Again the evangelist is apparently not interested in whether or not this has been taught to the disciples.

After the Feeding of the Five Thousand, Jesus walks on the waters ("I am" 14:22–27). Peter now attempts to come to him on the waters but fails and is rescued (14:28–32); this is a lesson in faith and Matthew uses his characteristic word ὀλιγόπιστε. The disciples in the boat now make a formal confession of faith, "Truly you are Son of God" (14:33). As in 13:16–17, the disciples do indeed understand.

In this section Matthew includes a few geographical notices. Jesus crosses the lake to a deserted place before the Feeding of the Five Thousand and is followed by crowds (14:13), he goes to "the other side" (east or northeast, 14:22), returns to Gennesaret (14:34), and after the bitter controversy over the clean and the unclean goes to the regions of Tyre and Sidon where he heals the daughter of the Canaanite woman (15:21–28), and sails to Magadan (15:39). Now comes the discourse on the leaven, which the disciples understand after Jesus explains it to them (16:5–12). After this, he and his disciples go to the region of Caesarea Philippi, which like Tyre and Sidon is pagan territory.

The scene at Caesarea Philippi (16:13–28) contains much of the material found in the parallels, Mark 8:27–9:1 and Luke 9:18–27, but there are striking additions, notably the singular passage 16:17–19, in which Peter is congratulated and given special authority.

At this point I mention only a few phenomena. (1) Jesus' question to the disciples is,"Who do people say that the Son of Man is" (16:13; cf. Mark 8:27, "Who do people say that I am"; Luke 9:18, "Who do the crowds say that I am"). Here "Son of Man" can be only a self-designation anticipating the use of the phrase in vv. 27–28. (2) As in the other gospels, the Passion predictions begin at this point (16:21), but in this first one "Son of Man" does not appear; contrast Mark 8:31; Luke 9:22. (3) 16:27–28 reads, "For the Son of Man is going to come in the glory of his Father with his holy angels, and then he will reward everyone according to his doings. Truly, I tell you, there are some standing here who will not experience death until they see the Son of Man coming in his kingdom." The ideas that the Son of Man will judge and that he has a kingdom match the teachings of the parable of the Weeds and the Seine, and are absent from the parallels, Mark 8:38–9:1 and Luke 9:26–27.[11]

This pericope is a turning point in the gospels of Matthew and Mark, a little less obviously in Luke. From this point on, the story points toward the Passion. It is here also that Peter makes his Christological statement, "You are the Messiah, the Son of the living God" (16:16), and Jesus answers, "Blessed are you, Simon Barjona, because flesh and blood has not revealed it to you, but my Father who is in the heavens" (16:17). One may contrast this with Mark 8:27–33, in which Jesus bids the disciples to be silent and goes on to speak of the suffering of the Son of Man (cf. also Luke 9:13–22). Matthew, like Mark, records Peter's rejection of the idea that Jesus must suffer (16:22–23), but this comes only after the blessing on Peter, who has correctly discerned part of the mystery.[12]

One may speak of a"messianic secret" in Mark, but in Matthew it is a secret withheld from the outsiders, not from the disciples. Beginning with the Sermon on the Mount, signs of Jesus' divinity appear both in his acts and his words, and the disciples give him something like divine honor. Thus in Matthew the Caesarea Philippi pericope is a climax and summary of what goes before, not a new revelation. In contrast to Mark,

---

[11] Cf. C. H. Talbert and E. V. McKnight "Can the Griesbach Hypothesis be Falsified?" *JBL* 91 (1972) 344–53.

[12] It may be argued that Matthew is more severe than Mark because he calls Peter a σκάνδαλον (16:23), but this noun, usually in the plural, is a favorite with Matthew; he also uses the verb σκανδαλίζω more frequently than the others.

there is no pattern in the Son of Man sayings up to this point. Here the first explicit Passion predictions begin, as in the parallel section in Mark, but even this has been anticipated by the reference to the Servant of Yahweh (8:17; 12:17–21), the implication that when the disciples are persecuted it is no more than that which Jesus suffered (10:24–25), and especially by the veiled reference to Jesus' death and resurrection in the Sign of Jonah saying (12:40).

Matthew's interpretation of Jesus as Son of God, Messiah, Son of Man and Servant is homogeneous throughout the gospel. This is discussed further in Chapter 7.

The Transfiguration

When one asks how Matthew connects the Caesarea Philippi pericope with the Transfiguration (17:1–18), it would seem, in view of the promises made in 16:28, that the evangelist thinks of this event on the high mountain as a preliminary vision of the Son of Man in his kingdom. One does not, however, find the symbolic arrangements of Mark's gospel; i.e., the disciples fail to understand Jesus' words about the bread and the leaven (Mark 8:14–21); the blind man of Bethsaida is healed in two stages (8:22–26); the disciples' eyes are partially opened, they gain (or should have gained) an understanding of Jesus' nature and purpose (8:27–9:1); and they see him transfigured and hear the voice from heaven (9:2–8). Matthew has no healing of a blind man at this point. He does have a discourse on the leaven, and the disciples understand (Matt 16:12).

As in Mark 9:9–13, there is a discussion as the company descends the mountain (Matt 17:9–13), but again the disciples understand. The GH demands that Mark has rewritten the entire section Matt 16:5–17:13 to heighten the stupidity of the disciples. But there is some lack of comprehension, which continues in the story of the epileptic boy (Matt 17:14–20 = Mark 9:14–29). Luke handles this entire part of the gospel story somewhat differently.

In all three gospels the second Passion prediction follows the story of the epileptic. At this point it is only Matthew who includes the dialogue on the Temple tax (17:24–27). The disciples are free from this obligation, but they should pay the tax in order to avoid criticism. This was advice useful for a congregation in close relation to a Jewish community. If in Matthew's time the tax was collected by the Roman government, paying it would serve as a protection against persecution.

Rules for the Church

The discourse which concludes Matthew's fourth book (Chap. 18) will be discussed later when the three gospels are compared as to their legal teaching and ecclesiology. The point to be noticed here is that it contains precepts for governance of the Church (here thought of as embodied in a local congregation), so much so that it has been called the beginnings of canon law. The central part gives a rule for adjustment of personal disputes which develops the biblical principle of two or three witnesses and provides for excommunication in extreme cases (18:15–17). The authority to bind and loose is restated (18:18; cf. 16:19). This is strengthened by a saying originally referring to prayer together with the promises that Christ will be present where two or three are gathered in his name (18:19–20). This last has a parallel in one of the most beautiful of all rabbinic sayings (*m. 'Abot* 3:2).

All of this is framed by (*a*) three pericopes at the beginning; the saying that one must become like children, i.e., must accept the humble and low status of children; sayings on scandals to "little ones," the more immature and weak members of the Church; and the parable of the Lost Sheep; and (*b*) the dialogue with Peter which introduces the parable of the Unforgiving Slave (18:21–35). It is in the light of this that the Church must exercise discipline.

The Climax of the Public Ministry

The final section before the Passion Narrative (19:2–26:2) is basically eschatological, though it contains other elements, and its colophon is a fourth Passion prediction (26:1–2) which introduces what follows.

The narrative portion of this (19:2–23:29) consists of two parts: teachings and incidents when Jesus is on the east side of the Jordan and in Jericho as he is on his way to Jerusalem (19:2–20:24) and an account of Jesus' activities and teachings in Jerusalem (Chaps. 21–23). Thus Matthew continues to follow his loose geographical framework.

The first item is the divorce pericope (19:3–9), which was anticipated in 5:31–32 and which comes logically after the legal material in Chap. 18. A dialogue on "eunuchs" (19:10–12) is appended. Most of the rest is instruction for the twelve disciples as to their behavior and attitudes. Even the parable of the Laborers in the Vineyard (20:1–16), peculiar to Matthew, seems to be placed where it is because Jesus has just spoken of rewards, and the evangelist uses it to reinforce the teaching that the first shall be last (19:30; 20:16). There is a third Passion prediction, and as the company leaves Jericho a second healing of two blind men (20:29–34; cf. 9:27–31).

After Jesus arrives at the Mount of Olives the stories of Jesus' public ministry in Jerusalem parallel to a large degree the corresponding parts of Mark and Luke. There are, however, two parables at this point not found in the other gospels. The Great Supper (22:1–14) appears in Luke in a different form at 14:15–24. The Two Sons (21:28–32) expresses a familiar theme of Matthew, that performance not words brings acceptance, and Matthew uses this to contrast those who rejected John the Baptist (11:16–19) with the believing tax collectors and harlots. In this way he anticipates 23:3.

23:1–36 is a self–contained discourse which brings the controversies of Chaps. 21–22 to a climax. It is basically a series of woes or curses addressed to "scribes and Pharisees, hypocrites" which reminds one of the comminations in the 1662 English Prayer Book (which of course is based on Deut 27:15–26).

The first part of the accompanying discourse is in Chap. 24, which will be discussed later. This predicts the destruction of the Temple, the woes and tribulations of the end-time, the coming of the Son of Man, and at the end pericopes which teach that no one can know the day or the hour and demand watchfulness and obedience. This last (24:36–51) has parallels in parts of Luke 12 and 17. The reward of the faithful slaves and judgment on the unfaithful leads directly to the three parables of Chap. 25, all of which give eschatological tension the same moral basis; it is deeds, not words, that count. The parables of the Ten Young Girls and the Talents are directed primarily to Christians; 25:31–46 declares that the Son of Man will judge people of all nations on the same basis.

The Passion and Resurrection

The Passion Narrative contains nearly all the material in Mark's narrative and most of that in Luke. There are, however, pericopes and verses not found elsewhere, notably the death of Judas (27:3–10) which concludes with a formula citation employing Zech 11:12–13:1; Jer 32:6–9; the dream of Pilate's wife (27:19); portents at the time of the Crucifixion (27:51–53) and the guard at the tomb (27:62–66).

There are three resurrection scenes. The women find the tomb empty and an angel directs them to tell the apostles to go to Galilee, where they will see the risen Lord. After this Jesus himself meets them and repeats the command to go to Galilee (18:11–15), the eleven disciples are reunited with Jesus on the mountain in Galilee and commissioned to evangelize all nations. The commission (28:19–20) sums up Matthew's teaching: the Eleven are commanded to make disciples, baptize and teach all that Jesus has commanded (e.g., the Sermon on the Mount). He is to be with them always till the close of the age, the risen Lord ruling over his Church (cf. 18:20).

The Structure of Matthew

Matthew has an outline that tells the story of Jesus' ancestry, conception, birth and infancy, and carries the narrative of his ministry from his baptism to the Cross and Resurrection. This is developed with much typology and fulfillment of prophecy in which the evangelist uses a unique formula for citations. This story line is crossed by a subsidiary pattern of narratives (which include teachings), each of which concludes with a discourse and a colophon. The evangelist's subsidiary purpose is catechetical. There is considerable emphasis on law and obedience and the Church's authority which stems from the presence of the risen Christ.

How useful this proved to be to the Church can be seen in the large use of Matthew made in most traditional lectionaries. For example, the old Armenian lectionary lists 27 readings from Matthew, 22 from John, 16 from Luke, and four from Mark.[13]

This study tends to show that Matthew has adapted materials from Mark so as to produce a gospel of a very different sort. In the next chapter I shall turn to Luke; and here, if the GH is correct, the third evangelist has produced a gospel entirely different from Matthew in plan, content and theology. It is easier to suppose that Luke has built this up, with much use of Mark, than that he has revised Matthew so radically.

---

[13] See John Wilkinson, *Egeria's Travels in the Holy Land* (rev. ed.; Jerusalem: Ariel, 1981) 262–75.

CHAPTER THREE

The Shape and Theology of Luke

Luke, like Matthew, has traits of a sacred history. The style and content of the first two chapters show a desire to link in with the LXX, which is now the Bible of most of the Church. Like Matthew, Luke is a supplement or companion to the "law of Moses and the prophets and the psalms" (24:44), although the prologue (1:1–4) in its relative modesty makes the claim that the author is writing only an "account." But it is also true that the prologue, the reference to Quirinius (2:2–3), and above all the synchronism in 3:1–2, integrate this into world history.

The evangelist thus has one eye on educated outsiders, but as in all apologetic works his principal interest and audience are the Christian community. In a sense his gospel is a "life of Jesus," even more than Matthew's gospel, and it is composed as the first volume of a history of Christian beginnings.

The Structure

In one respect Luke's gospel is shaped like that of Matthew, in that it has an account of Jesus' conception, birth and childhood, and narratives of the resurrection appearances. Otherwise its structure is very different even at the beginning, for after the prologue Luke recounts the annunciation of the birth of John the Baptist. In this connection it is significant that Peter's speech in Acts 10:34–43 is actually a good summary of Luke's gospel, and the word (λόγος, 10:31; ῥῆμα, 10:37, i.e., the message or gospel) begins from Galilee after the message that John preached.

Hans Conzelmann's study, *Die Mitte der Zeit* (The Center of Time), is a brilliant analysis of the structure of the two books, though it is possible to argue about some details. The first two chapters of Luke, at least, belong to the preceding age of the law and the prophets. Jesus' ministry is the center of time, and this consists of three stages: (1) the period when witnesses are gathered in Galilee, (2) the journey of the Galileans to the Temple, and (3) the period of Jesus' teaching in the Temple, the Passion, the Resurrection, and the Ascension. Then follows the age of the Holy Spirit and the Church.[1]

Luke as a Hellenistic Historian

At the same time Luke is something of a Hellenistic historian, as everyone has recognized since the work of Henry Cadbury.[2]

Thucydides was the primary model for Hellenistic historians. The first portions of his *History of the Peloponnesian War* are usually known as his *archaeologia*, the partly legendary history of Greece up to his time. Then at ii.2 he gives the famous synchronism which dates the incident leading to outbreak of the war. Whether consciously or not, Luke follows this pattern. Thus Chaps. 1–2 of the gospel can be considered his *archaeologia* in the sense that they refer to the age preceding Jesus' ministry. They are followed by the synchronism in 3:1–2.

Luke's traits as a Hellenistic historian go far beyond the *archaeologia* and the synchronism at the beginning of Chapter 3. One of the most recent studies, that of C. H. Talbert, shows that in so far as we can find a model for Luke's work, the most likely candidate is Diogenes Laertius' *Lives of Eminent Philosophers*. This of course was written later than Luke's time, but Diogenes' methods can be traced in earlier biographies.[3] This seems to remove Luke to some distance from primitive Christianity, yet Talbert's study of the architecture of the two documents and the intricate inner structure of Luke-Acts is persuasive. I suppose that it is the *content* of Luke and its roots in the OT monotheism that have hindered many scholars from seeing the resemblance to ancient biographies.

Yet this observation does not destroy the character of Luke as gospel. Kerygma does not have to be expressed in formulae of proclamation. Luke's gospel as a whole proclaims Jesus, and it has a distinct Christology which the original readers could have apprehended. Talbert remarks that a scholar "is able to see that the overall picture of Jesus is a

---

[1] H. Conzelmann, *The Theology of St. Luke* (New York: Harper, 1960) especially 16–17.

[2] H. J. Cadbury, *The Making of Luke–Acts* (New York: Macmillan, 1927).

[3] C. H. Talbert, *Literary Patterns, Theological Themes, and the Genre of Luke-Acts* (Missoula, MT: Scholars Press, 1974), especially Chap. VIII. In his later work, *What Is A Gospel?* (Philadelphia: Fortress, 1977) 124–27, Talbert discusses four examples of ancient biographies and shows why Diogenes Laertius was chosen for study.

theological rather than a strictly historical entity."[4] Both Luke and Mark, furthermore, had to oppose a mistaken or distorted Christology, a misuse of the gospel tradition,[5] and this we shall have to consider later. As examples of kerygma in Luke, one may think of Jesus' sermon at Nazareth (4:17–21), his answer to John the Baptist (7:22–23), the Beatitudes (6:20–23), "If I by the finger of God" (11:20), and Jesus' rejoicing (10:21–24). It may be objected that these are mainly soteriological rather than Christological, and proclaim the gospel *of* Jesus (the Reign of God) rather than the gospel *about* Jesus; nevertheless they imply a Christology.

The parallels to Diogenes Laertius bring us into the realm of the θεῖος ἀνήρ tradition. It is now widely understood that the Hellenistic world knew of many heroes, sons of gods, divine men, including kings, philosophers and various cult heroes, and that this had some influence on the way in which early Christians proclaimed the gospel. The claim is sometimes made that not only did Luke "historicize" the message, but also went further than Mark and Matthew in portraying Jesus as θεῖος ἀνήρ.[6] But this is mostly a matter of degree and emphasis. It is not so

---

4 Talbert, *Literary Patterns*, 111–12.

5 Talbert, *What Is a Gospel?* 120–22.

6 For Luke, see N. Perrin and D. C. Duling, *The New Testament: An Introduction* (New York: Harcourt Brace Jovanovich, 1982) 295–96. H. D. Betz, "Jesus as Divine Man," in *Jesus and the Historian* (ed. F. T. Trotter; Philadelphia: Westminster, 1968) 114–33. Betz finds the divine man Christology primarily in Mark. In Luke it is confined to the center of time, the period of salvation, 4:13–22:3 (126). The literature on the genre of the gospels and the divine man motif is immense. P. D. Shuler, "The Genre of the Gospels and the Two Gospel Hypothesis," in *Jesus, the Gospels, and the Church* (ed. E. P. Sanders; Macon, GA: Mercer University Press, 1987) 69–88, argues that all of the gospels have the genre of encomium biographies. This is essentially a secular genre, although the gospels have often been compared with Philostratus' *Life of Apollonius of Tyana* since the publication of the article bv C. W. Votaw, "The Gospels and Contemporary Biographies," *AJT* 19 (1915) 45–73, 217–49. The term θεῖος ἀνήρ became technical in history of religions studies through the work of L. Bieler, ΘΕΙΟΣ ΑΝΗΡ (2 vols.; Darmstadt: Wissenschaftliche, 1967). A partial bibliography of more recent studies is given by W. H. Kelber, *The Oral and the Written Gospel* (Philadelphia: Fortress, 1983) 81–82, n. 11. For the debate as concerns the gospels, see *The Aretalogy used by Mark: Protocol of the Sixth Colloquy of the Center for Hermeneutical Studies in Hellenistic and Modern Culture* (ed. W. Wuellner; Berkeley, CA: Center for Hermeneutical Studies, 1978), especially Morton Smith's paper, 1–22; also Smith's article, "Prolegomena to a Discussion of Aretalogies, Divine Men, the Gospels, and Jesus," *JBL* 90 (1971) 174–99. The hypothesis that the figure of Jesus as divine was due to the influence of Hellenistic religion had already been developed by W. Bousset, *Kyrios Christos* (Nashville: Abingdon, 1970). Although *Apollonius of Tyana* is often

often noticed in Matthew because that evangelist uses Jewish Christian language redolent of the OT, but he consistently invests Jesus with the traits of divinity. The θεῖος ἀνήρ portrayal in Mark is found particularly in the first half of that gospel. One question to be answered is its function in Mark and Luke.

Luke's Pre-History

With these considerations in mind, we may attempt an analysis of Luke's story line. In the first two chapters especially, comparisons with Matthew are inevitable. Perhaps the subtle difference in genre between Matthew and Luke can be expressed in this way. Matthew is a quasi-biblical piece, as some of the Kethubim, e.g., Chronicles-Ezra-Nehemiah, were when first composed, while Luke is more of a *companion to Scripture*.

In Chaps. 1–2, Luke is like Matthew in affirming that Jesus is descended from David (1:32–33). Later he gives a genealogy independent of Matthew which expresses Jesus' solidarity with the entire human race by tracing his descent back to Adam the son of God (3:23–28). He is also Son of God in another sense, born of a virgin, and Savior. The two cycles of John and Jesus, in fact the entire first two chapters, are told in a style reminiscent of the LXX. Luke also employs typology; e.g., the growing to manhood of John (1:80) and Jesus (2:52) reminds one of Samson (Judg 13:24–25) and Samuel (1 Sam 2:26). Luke is unique in including hymns or canticles reminiscent of the canonical Psalms and the Psalms of Solomon. It is also significant that important scenes take place in the Temple, which Jesus calls his Father's house (2:49).

Luke now matches Matthew in giving an account of John's preaching and the baptism of Jesus. The genealogy looks superficially like an excursus, but it has a definite function in his theology.[7]

Luke's Account of Jesus' Ministry

The account of the Temptation immediately precedes Jesus' arrival in Galilee "in the power of the Spirit" (cf. 3:22). Unlike Matthew and Mark,

---

cited as a model, the figure of Moses in Philo's *Life of Moses* stands near to the NT thought world. The appropriateness of the term θεῖος ἀνήρ as applied to Jesus has been questioned, but this does not affect the fact that the earthly Jesus is often presented in glorified form.

[7] See William S. Kurz, "Luke 3:28–38 and Greco-Roman and Biblical Genealogies," in *Luke-Acts: New Perspectives from the Society of Biblical Literature* (ed. C. H. Talbert; New York: Crossroad, 1984) 169–87.

Luke does not mention his proclamation of the Kingdom at this point; he will allude to this in 4:43.

Nevertheless the "center of time" begins here. What went before was the old era, and this time of salvation will be followed by the age of the Holy Spirit and the Church; Jesus' fame spreads and he is "teaching in their synagogues, glorified by all" (4:15).

Jesus now comes to the Synagogue of Nazareth on the sabbath and preaches from Isa 61:1–2; 58:6. The "favorable year of the Lord" may be the jubilee year; in effect it is part of what will be when the Kingdom arrives. But, in contrast to Matthew's structure, the people in his home village reject him at the very beginning of his ministry. This is programmatic; the message is destined to go to others.[8] The villagers intend to throw Jesus down over the cliff. Perhaps the first indication of Jesus' divine power is that he passes through the midst of them and goes his way.

The first miracle is the healing of a man with an unclean spirit (4:31 37) which is paralleled in Mark 1:21–28 but not in Matthew (except that the introduction appears in 7:28–29). Then follows the healing of Simon's mother–in–law, but we are not told who Simon is. Since Luke has said that "many" have previously undertaken to give an account of the "matters accomplished among us," does he suppose that this story is well known? Other people are now healed, the demons are commanded to be silent because they know that he is the Messiah, and Jesus withdraws elsewhere to preach the Kingdom (4:38–44).

From this point through Chap. 7, Luke's order of events diverges frequently from that of the other gospels. Where there is a common order, it is often like that of Mark. He tells of the exorcism in Capharnaum, various healings, and a preaching tour. But in place of the calling of the first four disciples, which appeared earlier in the other gospels, he now recounts the miraculous catch of fish (5:1–11) when Simon, James, and John are called. The next episodes (5:12–6:11) have parallels in Mark 1:40–3:6, but the corresponding parts of Matthew are in 8:1–4; 9:1–17; 12:1–14. The call of the Twelve (6:12–16) is at a point which does not correspond to its location in either of the other gospels. It is followed by a summary section (6:17–19) whose counterpart in Mark precedes the call of the Twelve.

If one proceeds on the basis of the GH, and supposes that Luke is editing Matthew, he has had to borrow some wording from Matt 4:24–25 after having lifted pericopes from Matt 8, 9, and 12. Then, according to

---

[8] R. H. Lightfoot, *History and Interpretation in the Gospels* (New York: Harper, 1935) 182–205.

the GH, Mark must have edited Matthew in composing 1:14–20 but afterward followed Luke's order, though not consistently. The latter is more plausible than Luke's adaptation of Matthew in this part of the gospel. The 2DH appears to be a more satisfactory solution of the phenomena, and Tuckett has pointed out the difficulties of the GH here.[9]

Matthew's Sermon on the Mount came approximately at the beginning of Jesus' ministry. The Sermon on the Plain (6:20–49) is, however, postponed to this point.

Luke's Sermon, since it follows a summary section, might seem to introduce an important section of the gospel. Jesus looks up at his disciples (6:20), but this is purely editorial; the discourse is designed for a wider audience. It begins with four beatitudes and four woes. The good news is for the poor (cf. 4:18), and most of the rest has to do with personal relations; the interest in law and cult, visible in Matthew's Sermon, is absent; this is the higher ethic or morality.[10]

Luke now tells of the healing of the Centurion's servant (7:1–10), a pericope that also comes after Matthew's Sermon (8:5–13), the raising of the young man of Nain (7:11–17), an important passage on John the Baptist (7:18–35), the forgiveness of the sinful woman (7:36–50), and the account of the women who followed Jesus (8:1–3). Parallels to Mark begin only after this.

There might, however, be another pattern. Talbert observes that there are eight correspondences between 4:16 –7:17 and 7:18 –8:56.[11] These are not in the same order, but he notes that the conclusions of the two sections match. At the end of the first, 7:1–10, the healing of the Centurion's servant emphasizes faith, and in 7:11–17 the widow's son is raised from the dead; similarly the woman with the hemorrhage has faith, and Jairus' daughter is raised from the dead (8:49–56). The two sections also corre-

---

[9] C. M. Tuckett, *The Revival of the Griesbach Hypothesis: An Analysis and Appraisal* (Cambridge: Cambridge University Press, 1983) 34–36.

[10] C. H. Talbert and E. V. McKnight, "Can the Griesbach Hypothesis be Falsified?" *JBL* 91 (1972) 357–60 discusses some of the parallels in the Sermons of Matthew and Luke.

[11] Talbert, *Literary Patterns*, 39–44. This monograph is a very important contribution to the understanding of Luke's compositional strategy and its relation to his theological purpose. Talbert studies correspondences within the gospel itself, the Book of Acts, and between Luke and Acts. In addition to the passages mentioned here, cf. also 10:21–13:30 with 14:1–18:30 (51–56) and 9:1–48 with 22:7–23:16 (26–29). In all cases the pattern in Luke cannot be matched in the other gospels. Talbert presumes that Luke used Mark, Q, and other sources. In order to defend the GH it would be necessary to refute his detailed reasoning.

spond at the beginning. An examination of parallels shows that these patterns cannot have been derived from Matthew, and that if Mark used Luke he ignored them.

The Spread of the Good News

In addition to the structures that Talbert has perceived, there may be other themes. We have noted that in Nazareth Jesus was rejected by his own people. Now in 7:1–10 there is the first clear indication that the Good News is coming to the Gentiles.[12] When Jesus raises the young man of Nain, outsiders hail him as a great prophet (7:16). This is followed by a composite section on John the Baptist (7:18–35). Both Jesus and John are rejected prophets. The passage also contains the theme of the old age and the new, which is frequent in Luke (7:28).[13]

Not only does the power of the gospel come to Gentiles, it is also for outcasts (7:34; cf. 5:27–32) and for women; a sinful woman is forgiven (7:36–50), and Jesus has many women disciples (8:1–3). Here I perceive a gradual widening of the outreach of the Good News. Later Jesus will go to Samaritans.

In the parables section, 8:4–18, Luke reproduces much of the substance of Matt 13:1–23 and Mark 4:1–25 in brief form, but the content is closer to Mark than to Matthew. Parallels to 8:16–17 (= Mark 4:21–24) are found in other parts of Matthew's gospel. Luke (8:9–10) does not seem to be as interested as Matthew (13:10–17) and Mark (4:10–12) in the hiding of the knowledge of God's Kingdom from outsiders; the emphasis is therefore on disclosure of the secret (8:16–17). The rest of Chap. 8 consists mostly of miracles, told in the same order as that of Mark, with one exception. Contrary to the order in the other two gospels, Luke places the visit of Jesus' family (8:19–21) after the parable of the Sower rather than before.

Jesus' Nature Revealed to the Twelve

The next section, 9:1–50, completes the gathering of the witnesses in Galilee and seems to be focused on the Twelve and their experiences in company with Jesus. The order is like that of Mark; Matthew's order cor-

---

[12] Talbert (*Literary Patterns*, 16–19) notes the correspondence between this and the conversion of the centurion Cornelius in Acts 10.

[13] The theme occurs in a different context in Luke 16:16, but Matt 11:11–14 brings the two sayings together. It is easier to explain this phenomenon by the 2DH than by the GH; cf. Tuckett, *Griesbach Hypothesis*, 148–57.

responds only in part. The Twelve are sent out on mission. Then there is a brief pericope on Herod Antipas (9:7–9). As in the other gospels the question of Jesus' identity prepares for Peter's confession (9:18–20). But Luke is not interested in the death of John the Baptist, which Matthew and Mark recount in such detail, perhaps as a counterpart to Jesus' Passion. Here he merely mentions John's death, as in 3:20 he had alluded to his imprisonment. In Matt 11:2, John is in prison when he sends disciples to Jesus; this is not mentioned in Luke 7:18. Here Luke's interest is in Herod, not John.[14]

The Feeding of the Five Thousand (9:10–17) leads immediately to Peter's confession and the discourse embodying the first Passion prediction (9:18–20, 21–27). Luke says only that this was in a place where Jesus had been praying alone; his readers would therefore assume that this was in Galilee.

The great "Lucan omission" (Mark 6:45–8:26 = Matt 14:22–16:12) comes between the feeding pericope and Peter's confession. There has been more than one attempt to explain this: (1) Luke had a mutilated copy of Mark. This is possible, but the items omitted are significantly coherent. (2) Luke may not have been interested in Jesus' activity in pagan territory because he had other ways of validating the Gentile mission. (3) The discourse on the leaven (Mark 8:14–21 = Matt 16:5–12) was obscure, and the theme of the disciples' stupidity (Mark 6:51) is not prominent in Luke. Nor was he as much interested in controversies over the law (Mark 7:1–23 = Matt 15:1–20) as the other evangelists. (4) Finally, the feeding of the Four Thousand (Mark 8:1–10 = Matt 15:32–39) largely duplicates the previous miracle, and other apparent doublets can be seen in the omitted material. Luke, as it stands, is the longest of all four gospels, and one can see that at many points Luke has abbreviated and this may be because of lack of space.

This last remark explains Luke's redactional method in the Caesarea Philippi pericope (9:18–27), but only partially. If he has been using Matthew he deliberately omits the verses which make Peter the Church's rock (Matt 16:17–19), but Peter's rebuke and Jesus' counter-rebuke (Matt 16:22–23 = Mark 8:32–33) are also lacking. In 9:26–27 he is closer to Mark 8:38, 9:1 than to Matt 16:27–28. The GH would presume that Luke has re-

---

14 Talbert, *Literary Patterns*, 26–29; again in 23:6–16, Antipas is glad to see Jesus. At the Last Supper, when Jesus speaks of eating and drinking at his table in the Kingdom of God (22:30), this corresponds to the feeding of the Five Thousand (9:12–17).

cast Matthew at this point and that Mark has followed his lead, but the 2DH provides a better explanation.[15]

Luke's form of the Transfiguration story (9:28–36) is singular in two respects. Moses and Elijah speak to Jesus of the "exodus" which he is to complete in Jerusalem (9:31). The "cloud" (singular, 9:34) corresponds to the cloud at the Ascension (Acts 1:9). Christopher Evans connects this "exodus" with the journey to Jerusalem that occupies 9:51–18:14.[16]

The next four pericopes, the exorcism of the epileptic boy, the second Passion prediction, the acceptance of children, and the exorcist who is not a disciple of Jesus (9:37–50), correspond to parallel passages in Mark. This last dialogue (9:49–50) has an ironic counterpart in the amusing story of the Jewish exorcists in Acts 19:11–16.

The Central Section

Luke's gospel now points toward the Ascension. This, rather than the Cross and Resurrection, is the climax. The Transfiguration and 9:51, not Peter's confession, mark the turning point of the gospel, in contrast to Matthew and especially to Mark. The Central Section, as everyone recognizes, is miscellaneous, and Evans' explanation is that it is structured on Chaps. 1–26 of Deuteronomy. This would be an amazing example of typology and the writing of sacred history.[17]

Other theological understandings of the Central Section are possible. W. C. Robinson, Jr., who considers that the travel section extends to 19:27, states that Luke visualized the continuity of the history of revelation as a δρόμος or ὁδός; cf. Acts 13:16–25. The trip is a stage on the Way of the Lord, and the function of the travel narrative is to serve Luke's

---

[15] Mark 9:1 exhibits traits of Mark's style; see Tables 13, 74, 89, 194 in D. B. Peabody, *Mark as Composer* (Macon, GA: Mercer University Press, 1987). But Matt 16:27b is just as clearly Matthaean, not only in the idea that recompense is according to one's deeds, but also in the use of καὶ τότε, and Matthew uses ἀποδίδωμι twelve times, Mark only once (12:17).

[16] C. F. Evans, "The Central Section in St. Luke's Gospel," in *Studies in the Gospels: Essays in Memory of R. H. Lightfoot* (ed. D. E. Nineham; Oxford: Blackwell, 1955) 37–53; see 51. It is, however, most important to account for the non-Marcan (or non-Matthaean) portions of the section.

[17] Vincent Taylor, "The Original Order of Q," in *New Testament Essays in Memory of T. W. Manson* (ed. A. J. B. Higgins; Manchester: Manchester University Press, 1959) 246–69, argued that it is Luke, not Matthew, who generally followed the order of Q. If one analyzes the passages cited by Evans, omitting the materials peculiar to Luke, the same pattern remains. Thus, if Luke was dependent on Q, he must have observed the pattern and added to it.

concept of authenticated witness. Christian witness is based on the testimony of witnesses who are accredited by (1) their presence during Jesus' Galilean ministry, (2) the fact that they follow him on the way to Jerusalem, and (3) their witness of the Resurrection.[18]

The Central Section from 9:51 up to 18:14 takes the place of Mark 9:41–10:12 or Matt 18:8–19:12, and together with the rest of the journey (Luke 18:15–43) provides an impressive training for both church leaders and Christians in general.[19]

The 2DH holds that Luke simply omitted the parts of Mark noted above. A careful review shows that in his Central Section he cannot be proved to have made use of Mark, although it is barely possible. Where parallels to Mark do exist one can argue that Luke is using Matthew or Q, and some of the parallels to Mark are distant; Mark appears to have material similar to Q or to one or both of the other gospels.[20]

---

[18] W. C. Robinson, Jr., "The Theological Context for Interpreting Luke's Travel Narrative (9:51 ff)," *JBL* 79 (1960) 20–31. See also Michi Miyoshi, *Der Anfang des Reiseberichts Lk 9:51–10:24: eine redaktionsgeschichtliche Untersuchung* (Rome: Pontifical Biblical Institute, 1974), reviewed by C. H. Talbert, *JBL* 95 (1976) 138–39. Miyoshi shows that this section has links both with earlier material in the gospel and with the portions of the Central Section that follow.

[19] Evans, "Central Section of St. Luke's Gospel," 51–53, argues that "Luke's principal source, Mark, not only provides a context for the insertion of such a section [the Central Section], but may well have suggested such a procedure" and that Mark 10:13–34 "furnishes an appropriate sequel to it." In itself this would fit in with the GH. The difference is that Matthew includes some materials not found in Mark.

[20] For example, the Sign of Jonah pericope (Luke 11:29–32) deals with the same issue as Mark 8:12 ("no sign shall be given this generation"), but there is no observable literary dependence. There is a parable of the Absent Master in Luke 12:35–38 which resembles the one at the end of Mark's apocalyptic discourse (Mark 13:33–37). Luke speaks of three watches of the night (Jewish reckoning), Mark of four watches (Roman). In Luke 17:22–37, verses 25, 31–33 break the context. Verse 32 (Lot's wife) is clearly due to Luke. 17:25 is probably the evangelist's summary of what he wrote in 9:22 (first Passion prediction); similarly, cf. 17:33 and 9:24. In 17:31 (the person on the roof) Luke could have borrowed from Mark 13:15–16, but the GH would hold the source to be Matt 24:17–18. Yet if Mark is dependent on one of the other gospels, why would he have changed the correctly grammatical ἐν (τῷ) ἀγρῷ to εἰς τὸν ἀγρόν and add μὴ εἰσελθάτω?

There are other pericopes in the Central Section that call for study which are independent of Mark but are an important part of the argument in favor of Q, e.g., 10:1–20 (mission and return of the Seventy-two); 10:25–28 (summary of the law), and 13:18–19 (parable of the Mustard–seed). Luke 10:1–20 is the evangelist's editing of various materials, some of which may be from Q. But 10:17–20 is not found in any other gospel. It includes Jesus' dramatic saying when the disciples return and say that the demons are subject to them. This would have been suitable for Mark's

Luke is vague on gospel geography, as one can see in the earlier part of his gospel. Nevertheless the Central Section contains a few indications of places. Jesus has apparently been in Galilee up to now but suddenly he appears at a Samaritan village (9:52). As a contrast to his rejection there, Jesus tells a parable of a Good Samaritan (10:30–37), but when he visits Martha and Mary one supposes that he is still in Galilee (10:38–42). The impression, then, is that he is on the borders of Galilee and Samaria. Later on he goes through cities and villages on his way to Jerusalem (13:22). He must be in or near Galilee when he hears of Herod's threat (13:31–33). Then in 17:11 he is on his way to Jerusalem διὰ μέσον (Leaney, "the border country";[21] RSV "between") Galilee and Samaria, where he heals ten lepers, one of whom is a Samaritan. Jesus is still on the way to Jerusalem when he utters the third Passion prediction (18:31–34). In the next pericope he and the disciples are approaching Jericho.

Most of the materials in the Central Section have no Samaritan setting whatever. Pharisees appear at 11:37, 14:1, 15:2, 17:20, cf. 10:25, 13:10. It is generally agreed that the journey is a literary device to include some of the most important materials Luke has at hand and to suggest a long journey in which Jesus teaches the disciples. Evans' theory is that this is Jesus' Deuteronomy (new law). If Luke was using Matthew, he deliberately ignored the statement that Jesus went into "the regions of Judaea beyond Jordan" (Matt 19:1). Likewise there is no mention of other parts of the Decapolis region (except for the Gergesene or Gerasene country, 8:26).

The Book of Acts shows great interest in geography, and since there are at least a few geographical references in the gospel, the evangelist must have had some mental picture of this journey. He knew of Samaria as important in the Christian mission (Acts 8:4–25), and could have imagined an itinerary from Galilee in which Jesus followed a wady to the Jordan Valley and approached Jericho from the west side of the river.[22]

Most of the parables in the Central Section are found only in Luke. There are sayings on many themes, but especially much material on dis-

---

purposes, particularly if he wished to emphasize the victory of the Reign of God. In Mark 6:12 the disciples cast out demons and Jesus has given them this authority (6:7) as he had not done in Luke 10:1–12. Mark, like Luke, tells of a successful exorcist who did not belong to the Twelve, and Jesus approves of his work (9:38–40).

21 A. R. C. Leaney, *The Gospel according to St. Luke* (London: Black, 1958) 227.

22 C. C. McCown, "The Geography of Luke's Central Section," *JBL* 57 (1938) 51–66. "Luke shows definite geographical knowledge only of the country between Caesarea Stratonis and Jerusalem" (55).

cipleship, opposition, controversy, and denunciation of opponents. There is one important section on prayer (11:1–13). The one directly Christological passage is 10:21–24 (=Matt 11:25–27). There are three miracles (actually four, 11:14). Two of these are related to the law (13:10–17, 14:1–5). Otherwise there is little attention to the law except in 16:14–18 and the denunciation of the lawyers (11:37–54). Eschatology is one of the leading elements (12:35–48, 54–56, 59–60; 13:1–9; 17:20–37 and a few other places). Jesus' disciples are in danger of death (12:4–5) but there are very few references to the death of Jesus except for his "being taken up" (9:51); Jesus' reference to fire and a future baptism (12:49–50), which makes one think of the ordeals of a hero; his response to Herod (a prophet must die only in Jerusalem, 12:33); and 17:25, which is like a Passion prediction and appears to be based on Matthew or Mark.[23]

The total effect of the Central Section is to build up the tension between Jesus and his opponents and to affirm that the eschatological crisis will surely come, but only when it is least expected (12:40, 17:26–30).

In considering the GH, it is necessary to explain why Luke might have drawn so many pericopes and sayings from Matthew and collected them in the Central Section.

Beginning with 18:15, Luke resumes the general outline of Matthew and Mark, but, as we have noticed, omits the pericope Matt 19:20–28 = Mark 10:35–45. He inserts the story of Zacchaeus (19:1–10) and the parable of the Pounds, into which another parable is intercalated (19:11–27).

The Ministry in Jerusalem and the Passion Narrative

The account of Jesus' ministry in Jerusalem follows the other two gospels in the main, except that the pericope of the Summary of the Law is omitted because a similar piece was included in the Central Section (10:25–28), where a "lawyer" gave the answer. The most striking differences are that all of Jesus' teaching is given in the Temple, and that the eschatological discourse (21:5–38) is completely recast so that the prophecy of the destruction of Jerusalem (21:20–24) is separated from the coming of the Son of Man.

The Passion Narrative in Luke differs so much from those in Matthew and Mark that it is often supposed that the evangelist had a

---

[23] R. H. Edwards, *A Theology of Q* (Philadelphia: Fortress, 1976), sees wisdom, prophecy and the eschatology of the Son of Man as the principal themes of Q. All of these are represented fully in the Central Section. He notes that Q has "a surprising lack in the saving significance of Jesus' death" (149). This, as one can observe in the Passion Narrative, is also characteristic of Luke himself.

special source or sources. Talbert has nevertheless recognized eight correspondences between 9:1–48 and 22:7–23:16.[24]

The Crucifixion is portrayed in a very different way. Jesus speaks like a prophet in his pathetic address to the daughters of Jerusalem (23:28–31). When Jesus is betrayed, the time of happiness and glory has come to an end, and Luke marks this by the words of Jesus, "This is your hour and the power of darkness" (22:53). The dying Lord does not shout Ps 22:1; the words from the Cross are "Father, forgive them" (23:34, textually insecure), the word to the penitent bandit (23:43), and his last word, a quotation of Ps 31:5 (23:46). Jesus' words are those of a king and the Son of God, confident in his relationship with the Father, almost like the Johannine Christ. This fits with the θεῖος ἀνήρ Christology observable elsewhere in the gospel. The centurion does not need to say that "this was a son of God;" that he is "righteous" (23:47) might mean merely that Jesus is innocent, but in this context it suggests that Jesus' death was like that of a philosopher-hero.

The Resurrection

The Resurrection stories in Luke differ radically from those in Matthew and Mark. The only Lucan pericope parallel to them is 24:1–11. Matthew and Mark say that a young man or an angel utters a message to the disciples that Jesus is preceding them to Galilee, where they will see him, and Matthew records his appearance on a mountain there. But in Luke there is no suggestion of any reunion in Galilee. What the "two men" say to the women is "Remember what he said to you *while he was still in Galilee*, that the Son of Man must be delivered over," etc. (24:6–7). The same δεῖ (ἔδει) appears in the Emmaus story; the Messiah must suffer and enter his glory, as the Scriptures teach (24:25–27). This interpretation of the Cross, that Messiah/Son of Man is the Servant of Yahweh who dies in obedience to God's will, appears again in the final commission to the Eleven (24:46); what is to be proclaimed is forgiveness

---

[24] Talbert, *Literary Patterns*, 26–29. In three of these instances there is new material. The pericope of the two swords is given an editorial introduction that harks back to 9:3. Jesus' covenant or testament of a kingdom (22:28–30) is either a special tradition or editorial; only verse 30 is paralleled in Matt 19:28. The hearing before Herod Antipas (23:6–16) has a counterpart in 9:9; it is only Luke who says that Herod desired to see Jesus. Talbert notes that in 9:20–22 and 22:31–34 Peter makes a confession immediately after a meal. This comes about because of Luke's structure; in Chap. 9 the confession follows immediately after the feeding of the Five Thousand. See also note 11 above.

through his name (24:47). The disciples are witnesses to this death and resurrection (24:49, Acts 1:8, 3:18–21).

As compared with Mark and Matthew, Luke guards against any possible suggestion of docetism by affirming the reality of the risen body of Jesus. Christ bids the disciples touch and feel him, and he eats a piece of broiled fish (24:39–43).[25]

Conclusions

This review of the gospel's structure shows that while it resembles that of Matthew at the beginning, Luke has built his gospel on a quite different plan. Orchard attempted to argue that, even in the Central Section, Luke has modelled his collection on Matthew's discourses, but Tuckett has answered this claim in detail.[26]

If, as the GH assumes, Mark has used both Matthew and Luke, he has ignored almost completely Luke's understanding of the course of Jesus' ministry; his basic structure is more like that of Matthew. In this case he has deserted Matthew's order of pericopes at various points in favor of that of Luke, and has inserted a few Lucan pericopes such as the exorcism in the Capharnaum synagogue (1:21–27 = Luke 4:31–33) and the Strange Exorcist (9:38–40 = Luke 9:49–50). One might add that he substitutes Luke's form of the exorcism story (8:26–39) and at 10:46–52 has a story similar to Luke 18:35–43 in place of corresponding parts of Matthew. But in all these cases, Mark appears to be primary and the other gospels secondary.

Beyond all this, Luke has a distinctive view of the purpose of Jesus' ministry. The Church that he sees emerging from it is for all nations— here he agrees with the other gospels—but it is more a missionary movement of liberation, the way of the Lord, than a community with a new law. Its first leaders are the Eleven or Twelve, but their circle is to be enlarged to include other apostles and evangelists. Like Matthew and Mark, he is able to think of the time before the end as relatively brief, yet

---

[25] D and some MSS of the OL omit v. 40. This and other textual variants in Chaps. 23–24 are discussed by George Rice, "Western Non-Interpolations: A Defense of the Apostolate," in *New Perpectives*, 1–16. Rice concludes that the omissions were a deliberate attempt to protect the reputation of the apostles by minimizing their unbelief. Thus v. 40 and other readings of the Alexandrian text appear to be the work of Luke. Although this evangelist tends to minimize this trait of the disciples, he reserves it to some degree.

[26] Tuckett, *Griesbach Hypothesis*, 37–40.

the future is more indefinite, and under men like Paul the Church is developing in the power of the Holy Spirit.

In order to go further, it is necessary to examine specific pericopes in the light of the GH and the 2DH, and particularly to compare the three gospels with respect to their basic theological themes—Christology, the Reign of God, Judaism and Law, and the Church.

CHAPTER FOUR

Mark as Story Teller and Writer

Mark in Relation to Other Literature

The judgment of K. L. Schmidt that the gospels are not "high literature" or *belles lettres*, but rather *Kleinliteratur*, popular writings, has been
generally accepted.[1] Schmidt, of course, did not mean that these books
were like present newspaper writing or the tracts that well-meaning
evangelists hand out. He was not making an aesthetic judgment but trying to determine a *Gattung*. No doubt there have been critics other than
St. Jerome, trained in the Greek and Latin classics, who have disdained
the style of biblical books, but the gospels in particular have not only
survived but—to state the obvious—have exercised power, not merely
because of their religious content but partly by their method of presenta-
tion.

Theologians have not often paid much attention to the aesthetic
aspect of biblical books, and appreciation of this has too often been left to
the professors of English literature or comparative literature. Everyone,
however, discerns the beauty of the Beatitudes, the parables of Jesus, and
1 Cor 13. Ernest Renan went so far as to call the Gospel of Luke "the most
beautiful book in the world." The loveliness of that gospel does not
change the fact that, although its author has some of the traits of a
Hellenistic historian, Luke is related to Mark in *genre*. Mark is without
pretensions to literary art as the Hellenistic world understood it, but his
gospel is far from being an artless collection of sayings and episodes
strung together. As for Paul's letters, recent research has disclosed the

---

[1] K. L. Schmidt, "Die Stellung der Evangelien in der allgemeinen
Literaturgeschichte," in *ΕΥΧΑΡΙΣΤΗΡΙΟΝ* (ed. H. Schmidt; Göttingen: Vandenhoeck
& Ruprecht, 1923) Part 2, 50–134.

rhetorical features in them. They were not dashed off but carefully constructed to produce a desired effect.[2]

One can also perceive a freshness in Paul's letters and in the gospels (especially in Mark), the freedom to write as impelled and controlled by the message to be expressed. It is not that there are no models, but Mark, Paul, and Luke were not bound by them. As Amos Wilder has said, the early Christians developed a rhetoric of their own, a fresh language, to express a gospel entirely new to the world.[3]

Some time ago it occurred to me that there are analogies between Mark and folk art. Later I hope to develop this idea, and at present I set down some tentative suggestions.

Folk art at its purest, and especially in its pre-literate stages, is the product of a rather self-contained, traditional culture. Here one may think of the early Celts, Norse, and Saxons, and the artifacts of the Scythians, Navajos, Hopi, Zuñi, and Polynesians; in words, the Yugoslav oral epics and the *Kalevala* of the Finns, some of the poetry of the OT, and the Arabic poetry of the desert.

All the traditional arts have this in common, that each has its own styles of structure, design, and ornamentation. The artifacts and writings are not mass-produced; they are the work of men and women who are craftsmen concerned for the materials and the forms into which they are worked. A man on the island of Bali is said to have explained to a European or an American that his people had no separate category that they called art. "We just like," he said, "to make everything beautiful."

Some of the finest literature in the world reflects the oral and more primitive stages of culture. The *Iliad* and the *Odyssey* were given their present form, probably in the 8th century B.C. by one or two great masters. But they contain materials and forms that go back to the Mycenaean period; they are on the edge of oral tradition and have blended elements

---

2 See, e.g., H. D. Betz, *Der Apostel Paulus und die sokratische Tradition* (Tübingen: J. C. B. Mohr, 1972); "The Literary Composition and Function of Paul's Letter to the Galatians," *NTS* 21 (1975) 353–79; W. Wuellner, "Greek Rhetoric and Pauline Argumentation," in *Early Christian Literature and the Classical Intellectual Tradition* (ed. W. R. Schoedel and R. L. Wilken; Paris: Beauchesne, 1977) 177–88.

3 A. N. Wilder, *The Language of the Gospel: Early Christian Rhetoric* (New York: Harper & Row, 1964), especially 9–25, 35–37. Long ago, Wilamowitz said "...this Greek of his (Paul's) is related to no school and follows no model. . . and yet is still just Greek, not a translated Aramaic. . . this makes him one of the classicists of Hellenism. At last, at long last one speaks again in Greek of a new experience of life." U. von Wilamowitz, *Kultur der Gegenwart*, quoted in J. Weiss, *Earliest Christianity* (New York: Harper, 1959) 2. 399–400.

of different times and cultures into an artistic whole. The Hellenistic world in which the gospels were composed, was not like 8th century Greece. Although most of the population was illiterate, a great body of literature existed. Mark was in close touch with oral tradition, but his purpose was to write and so to fix the story and to give it a theological interpretation. He quoted from the OT, he (or his sources) used parts of it as a model, e.g., the Elijah and Elisha cycles, and probably made some use of written sources.

In the sayings of Jesus we are nearer to folk art. The culture in which he lived was not entirely oral. Scripture was read in the synagogue; Jesus appears to have quoted it and perhaps knew many passages by heart; and Luke says that he read a pericope in the Nazareth synagogue. But Jesus did not write; his message was by word of mouth.

The Jews of Galilee, among whom he lived, had a coherent culture of their own, not identical with that of Jerusalem. The villagers and fishermen had some knowledge of the OT and the Jewish tradition; this formed their mental outlook to a degree. They must have had their own songs and dances, certainly they built their own houses, made their tools; many of the dishes and cooking pots must have been made locally. Since they had a material and spiritual culture, they must have had folk poetry also, some traditional, some made up for the occasion. Jesus himself was a poet. The parallelism of his sayings is like that of OT poetry. If the attempted retranslations into Aramaic made by Canon Burney, Ernst Lohmeyer, and Joachim Jeremias are at all close to the original words, one finds rhythm, assonance, and rhyme in the Beatitudes and to some extent in the Lord's Prayer. Even in Greek and English dress, the power of Jesus' rhetoric comes through. We may not hear the sound of the words, but the imagery is there.

The Social Setting of the Gospels

The gospels are to some degree removed from early first century Palestine. They belong in a Christian, not a purely Jewish setting. By now the early Christians were a distinct sociological group that was not cut off from the main streams of Judaism and Hellenism, but very soon they had to begin developing a new sub-culture in the midst of the majority cultures. This was because the power of the Good News had to be expressed both in words and in a style of life.

All of the gospels reflect the new rhetoric appropriate to this, and they drew on the oral tradition that Mark especially knew. Kelber, in his chapter on "Mark as Textuality,"[4] discusses what was lost in creativity and spontaneity and what was gained when the gospel took written form. Mark he believes, rejected the oral prophets who sometimes made extravagant claims for their revelations. But the tradition now became fixed and was necessarily restricted in the main to the text.

The Character of Mark's Composition

In the many discussions of the Synoptic problem, little attention seems to have been paid to oral characteristics in Mark and the double tradition (Q) material. It may be well, then, to consider Mark's habits of composition and to compare them with the style of Matthew and Luke.

E. V. Rieu, the classical scholar, in the introduction to his translation of the gospels, remarked that it is easier to feel the spell of Mark's writing than to see just how he achieved his effects.[5]

Perhaps I can say a little more. The breathless character of Mark's gospel may be due in part to the fact that he is so full of his message, but it comes partly from traits of style that are ultimately oral. Kelber notes, for example, the historical present, pleonasms, the frequent use of εὐθύς, πάλιν, καὶ ἐγένετο, paratactic καί, etc. "These devices insinuate the suddenness, urgency, and non-simultaneity of successive events. They line up episodes paratactically like beads on a string."[6]

As in the case of Luke, one cannot always tell how much of the charm and excitement is due to the skill of the evangelist and how much to his sources. Certainly Mark's concrete and vivid detail is one factor.

At Jesus' baptism the skies are torn open (1:10), the Spirit drives him into the desert, and he is with the wild animals (1:16–17). In order to bring the paralytic to Jesus, the men dig through the mud and thatch of the roof (2:4). Jesus looks around at the people who are seated in a circle (2:34). The stilling of the storm (4:35–41) contains information not found in the parallels. There were other boats on the lake; Jesus was in the stern sleeping on a cushion; and when he rebuked the wind and the sea he said, "Silence, shut up!" The five thousand who are fed sit on the grass as

---

4 W. H. Kelber, *The Oral and Written Gospel* (Philadelphia: Fortress, 1983) 90–139. For remarks on Mark's purpose, see 97–101.

5 E. V. Rieu, *The Four Gospels* (Baltimore: Penguin, 1953) xxii.

6 Kelber, *Oral and Written*, 54–70 (quotation from 65). There are other traits of oral composition in which all three gospels share. In each story there are only two principal characters, Jesus and another person or group (51). There is no characterization; while Jesus and Peter have some individuality, "none of the characters . . . is fully rounded, knowable human being" (69).

though they were so many garden plots (6:39-40); and when Jesus is arrested in the garden a young man in white flees and leaves his garment behind (14:51–52). One detail might not be important except to those who first read the gospel, i.e., that Simon the Cyrenian was the father of Alexander and Rufus (15:21).

It is curious to suppose that Mark, in telling of the death of John the Baptizer (6:17–29), should add so much to the account in Matt 14:3–12, which contains all the essential information. This is like a popular tale of goings-on in an oriental court, such as one might find in Herodotus or the Book of Esther. Mark may recount the story for its own sake, simply because he has access to it; or he may give it special prominence as a counterpart to the Passion of Jesus. Thus, although Mark is often concise, he can be accused of rambling on here and there.

The evangelist can make mistakes. He should have written "Ahimelech" instead of "Abiathar" (2:26), and he refers to Isaiah the prophet but immediately quotes Malachi (1:2).

John C. Meagher has used the story of the Gerasene demoniac (5:1–20), as an example of how a story or joke may be spoiled by a clumsy raconteur; at this point the usual rules of form criticism break down. He also cites the cursing of the fig tree (11:12–19) and the discourse in 8:11–21.[7] Not everyone may agree how clumsy Mark is in 5:1-20, for the story is exciting and effective. But certainly the pericope does not have the smoothness of form and conciseness that one finds in typical miracle stories such as Mark 7:32–37, 8:22–26. If the GH is correct, it is difficult to know why Mark made such changes as he did; more probably the peculiarities existed in the oral tradition.

The intricate fashion in which Mark constructs his gospel shows that any rambling is only occasional, and it disposes of the notion that he is quite artless. For example, Lohmeyer found many schemes of threes.[8]

---

[7] J. C. Meagher, "Die Form- und Redaktionsungeschickliche Methoden: The Principle of Clumsiness and the Gospel of Mark," *JAAR* 43 (1975) 459–72, especially 467–69; *Clumsy Construction in Mark's Gospel* (New York: Edwin Mellen, 1979) 67–74. Kelber, *Oral and Written*, 53 explains certain peculiarities of the pericope Mark 5:1–20 as due to early Christian storytellers who were anti-Roman and equated the "legion" with the swine that are drowned. Meagher could have included the healing of the epileptic boy (9:14–29). Whereas Matthew has a brief, coherent narrative, the point of which is that the disciples lack faith, and in Luke it is a straight miracle story, in Mark Jesus declares that the demon can come out only through prayer (9:29). The coupling of faith and prayer occurs also in 11:22–24.

[8] E. Lohmeyer, *Das Evangelium des Markus* (Göttingen: Vandenhoeck & Ruprecht, 1959) 5–6.

Chiasmus is frequent, as in both the OT and the NT. This form is psychologically natural and common in both oral and written composition. Willi Marxsen is correct in his observation that Mark is, so to speak, "written backwards;" i.e., themes in the latter part of the gospel are anticipated in the earlier portions.[9] This resumption of themes is characteristic of Paul's letters also. But in Mark there are so many patterns that there is a wide diversity in the outlines attempted in various commentaries and introductions.

Mark likes to set a scene. The disciples provide a boat for Jesus so that the crowds will not press on him (3:9) and the boat figures in 4:1 also. There is an elaborate introduction to the feeding of the Five Thousand (6:31–34), whereas Matthew and Luke are brief at this point. It is only Mark who prepares for the third Passion prediction by speaking of the awe felt by the disciples (10:32). The picture of Jesus and his disciples looking at the Temple area (13:1–4) is an effective introduction to the eschatological discourse.

Parallels to such passages in the other gospels are either lacking or less circumstantial. The transitions between pericopes in Matthew and Luke tend to he short and stereotyped (e.g., Mt. 9:2, 14, 18; 11:25; 12:22; 14:1; Luke 8:4, 40; 9:57; 10:38; 11:29; 13:10; 16:13; 17: la). Luke occasionally has something more elaborate (5:17) and he likes to picture Jesus at prayer (6:12; 9:18, 28; 11:1).

Mark expects his readers to pick up clues. The ancients were accustomed to hear allegories and metaphorical speech. Mark indicated that the allegorical method could be applied to parables in general (4:13, 33–34) and he interpreted the metaphor of the bridegroom for his readers (2:19–20). Thus he probably expected them to understand that receiving the kingdom of God like a little child (10:15) and the casting of a mountain into the sea through faith and prayer (11:23) were to be understood figuratively. He also bade his readers to interpret the "abomination of desolation" (13:14); his immediate audience may have understood it but we cannot identify it precisely.

All the gospels make the story of Jesus dramatic, but the remarks of Northrop Frye apply especially to Mark. Jesus is at one and the same time the hero of a romantic quest and the central figure in a tragedy, but the narrative ends as a divine comedy. All through it there is also irony: the blindness and stupidity of the disciples and of the Jewish leaders and

---

[9] W. Marxsen, *Mark the Evangelist* (Nashville: Abingdon, 1969) 32–33.

Pilate, who suppose that they have won.[10] First century readers of Mark could feel that they understood secrets hidden from the Twelve and from Jesus' enemies.[11]

All three gospels used traditional material which retained something of its original oral character and had a variety of styles and forms. This is particularly true of what is claimed to be Q material, and Kelber's remarks on Q are worth considering.[12] Since this is so, in deciding which of the gospels is earliest, several factors should be taken into account: the overall shape and purpose of each, the examination of specific passages, and certainly the phenomena of oral style.

Matthew and Luke do not lack drama, but they are more leisurely, and in Matthew the drama is slowed down and at times recedes into the background because of his frequent insertion of teaching material into the story. The author of Matthew was essentially a teacher and builder of a community, with a strongly moralistic outlook, and the catechetical interest is almost as strong as his proclamation of Good News. He wrote a smooth and generally correct *koine* without pretensions to "fine writing."

Luke was a more self-conscious artist than the others and something of a Hellenistic historian. He tended to use various styles, choosing in each case the one that he deemed suitable to the occasion; yet in transmitting sayings of Jesus he seems to have been fairly faithful to his sources and here their originally oral character shines through.

Perhaps it can still be believed that Mark made use of Matthew and Luke, but in that case there are certain consequences. Mark then turns out to be a powerful and independent evangelist who shaped his materials to his own purposes and was determined to express his theological point of view through a story with vivid details, a fine sense of the dramatic and a highly selective choice of Jesus' teachings. He would have to be a revisionist, disdaining the methods of Matthew and Luke and even features of their Christologies, and aiming perhaps to reach an audience of a different cultural level which was oriented to oral speech and its forms. Perhaps he himself had been an oral teacher for some time; this

10 N. Frye, *Anatomy of Criticism* (Princeton: Princeton University Press, 1971) 163–239. "The sense of tragedy as a prelude to comedy seems almost inseparable from anything explicitly Christian" (215). See also *The Great Code* (New York: Harcourt Brace Jovanovich, 1982).

11 Dramatic irony is particularly characteristic of Mark and John. Everyone recognizes this in Caiaphas' famous prophecy (John 11:49–56) and it is present in all the misunderstandings of the disciples and other characters.

12 Kelber, *Oral and Written*, 199–203.

may be so, whatever the sequence of the Synoptics. The GH scenario is possible, but it is much more likely that Mark is more primitive than the others, and that the other evangelists revised his work to make it acceptable to a wider audience.

CHAPTER FIVE

The Reign of God

❖⟶◗◖⟵❖

Matthew

In considering passages on the Reign of God, which is the central theme of Jesus' proclamation, I follow the order in which the GH presumes that the three gospels were written, namely Matthew, Luke, and Mark. I shall do the same in Chapter 7, because as the three gospels stand, the Reign of God is involved in Christology. It is impossible to separate the two themes completely.

Matthew ordinarily speaks of "the Kingdom of heavens," Luke and Mark of the Kingdom (or Reign) of God," although Matthew uses the latter wording in 12:28; 19:24; 21:3, 43. Perhaps in these instances he has derived the phrase from his sources. His usual usage, which avoids the name of God, would be normal in a Jewish milieu. The question arises whether it is Matthew who makes the pious change, or that Luke has changed Matthew's form and is followed by Mark.

The first mention of the Kingdom is in Matt 3:1, and here, curiously, it is John the Baptizer who first announces its imminence. Jesus echoes this in 4:17 after the story of the Temptation and Matthew's majestic statement on Galilee as the land of revelation (4:12–17). But the evangelist has previously shown that Jesus is God's Son and has implied that he is Messiah son of David in the genealogy and by the visit of the Magi. The Baptizer has also predicted a Coming One who will baptize with the Holy Spirit and fire, presumably a fire of judgment (3:11 = Luke 3:16). Jesus' rejection of the kingdoms of this world (4:8–10) implies that the Kingdom belongs to God, but Jesus has the closest possible relation to it.

The Beatitudes (5:3–12) promise the Kingdom of the heavens to the poor in spirit, the persecuted, etc. Supporters of the 2DH sometimes maintain that Matthew has built up these beatitudes from Q, which is better represented by Luke's more direct promises addressed to the poor (Luke 6:20–23). The answer to the GH might be that Luke has a separate source, in which no conditions are attached to the promises.

All three gospels, however, mention conditions for receiving, entering or inheriting the Reign of God (e.g., Matt 5:20; 18:3; 19:14, 23; Luke 18:16–17, 24; Mark 10:14–15, 23), and in these contexts the words "eternal life" are used interchangeably with "Reign of God" (Matt 19:3, 29; Luke 18:18, 30; Mark 10:17, 30). The Kingdom is not only eschatological but also has a heavenly aspect. Similarly, Matthew's form of the Lord's Prayer reads "Our Father in the heavens. . .may your Kingdom come, let your will be done, as in heaven, so on earth" (6:9–10), while Luke 10:2 has "Father. . .may your Kingdom come." Unless the 2DH is correct, Luke has eliminated the heavenly aspect; the Kingdom will be on earth. It has not arrived completely, and Jesus teaches his disciples to pray for it.

The Kingdom also takes the form of the messianic banquet (Matt 8:11–12 = Luke 13:28–29, in a different context; cf. the introduction to the parable of the Great Supper, Matt 22:2; Luke 14:15). Then, at the Last Supper, Jesus promises to drink wine with the disciples in the Kingdom of God (Matt 26:29 = Mark 14:25; cf. Luke 22:16).

More will be said later about the parables of the Kingdom. Here it is best to note certain peculiarities of Matthew. The parable of the Weeds is made into a complete allegory by its interpretation (13:36–43). The Son of Man has a kingdom which embraces heaven and earth but is distinguished from the Kingdom of the Father; cf. 25:31–46, the parable of the Last Judgment, in which the Son of Man is both king and judge, and Jesus' final statement, "All authority in heaven and upon earth has been given to me" (28:18).

The same authority is evidently expressed when Jesus promises that Peter will be the rock on which he will build his Church and will be given the keys of the Kingdom of the heavens (16:18–19). This passage will be discussed more fully in a later chapter.

Luke

In Luke 1:32 the angel Gabriel promises Jesus a Davidic-messianic kingdom that will last forever. This is one of the few passages in this gospel in which Jesus has a kingdom, but this is in the future (cf. 22:29–30), and Luke does not say that he has this as Son of Man. As in Matt 4:8–10, Jesus rejects the tempter's offer of the kingdoms of this world (Luke 4:9–12).

The Reign of God is a constant theme in Luke, and its proclamation is the principal task of the disciples (e.g., 9:1–2, 60; 10:9). The message of its coming is implied when Jesus announces the year of liberation in Nazareth (4:17–21) but he does not use the phrase until later he says that he must go to other cities to proclaim it, because he was sent for that purpose (4:43).

Most of the occurrences of "Kingdom of God" in Luke have parallels in Matthew or Mark or both, but there are a few instances in his special material or his editing. Thus he adds, "You go and announce the kingdom of God" (9:60) and includes the saying, "No one who has put his hand to the plow and looks back is fit for the Kingdom of God" (9:62). There are those who have left homes and families for the sake of the Reign of God (18:29; cf. Matt 19:29, "for the sake of my name," Mark 10:29, "for the sake of the gospel"). There is an added reference to the Kingdom in 22:18.

The Kingdom as Present

Matthew and Luke contain sparse but significant examples of sayings of Jesus indicating the presence of the Kingdom in his ministry. Whether the same idea is present in the parables of Mark has been a subject of debate.[1]

The famous verses are Matt 12:28 and Luke 11:20, "If I by the finger (Matthew, 'spirit') of God cast out demons, then the Reign of God has already come upon you" (ἔφθασεν ἐφ᾽ ὑμᾶς). The Seed parables, particularly the Mustard-seed (Matt 13:31–32 = Mark 4:30–32 = Luke 13:18–19) and the Leaven (Matt 13:33 = Luke 13:20–21) can be understood as teaching that the Kingdom is in process of being realized, but in the former the accent is on the future.

Luke has another possible reference to the presence of the Kingdom: οὐκ ἔρχεται. . .μετὰ παρατηρήσεως. . .ἰδοὺ γὰρ ἡ βασιλεία τοῦ θεοῦ ἐντὸς ὑμῶν ἐστιν (17:20–21). This is interesting, first, because it precedes the Son of Man sayings but is separate from them. The two types of sayings belong to separate strands of tradition.[2]

---

[1] The most significant proponent of realized eschatology was C. H. Dodd, *The Parables of the Kingdom* (3rd ed.; New York: Scribners, 1951). He later agreed in principle with Jeremias' phrase "eschatology in process of realization." W. H. Kelber's work, *The Kingdom in Mark* (Philadelphia: Fortress, 1974), essentially extrapolates from Mark 1:14–15 so that all of Jesus' ministry involves the activity of the Kingdom.

[2] Philipp Vielhauer has discussed this phenomenon; cf. "Gottesreich und Menschensohn in der Verkündigung Jesu," *Aufsätze zum Neuen Testament* (Munich: C.

Mark and Luke put the two types of sayings side by side, and it is only Matthew who conflates them. Second, in the underlying Aramaic the saying in 17:20–21 might not have had a copula corresponding to ἐστίν, but Luke by using the present tense seems to say that the Kingdom is now "among you" or perhaps "within your grasp." Finally, by collocating the two traditions Luke implies either that the coming of the Son of Man will completely establish the Kingdom or that the presence of the Kingdom guarantees his future coming in judgment. Mark does not contain the saying just mentioned.

The GH holds that Luke has used Matthew. If so he treats the theme of the Reign of God with great independence, particularly in the crucial matters of the Beatitudes and the Lord's Prayer. The most important task of the disciples is to join him in proclaiming the Kingdom (cf. the mission of the Seventy-two, Luke 10:9–11), whereas in Matt 10:1, 8 the emphasis is on healing and exorcism, and in the charge of the Twelve the Kingdom is mentioned only in 10:7. Only in Matthew does Jesus have a kingdom as Son of Man.

Gehenna-Heaven Eschatology

The eschatology of the Synoptics is predominantly a time-eschatology (now/then; this age/the age to come); but there is evidence that early Christians, like Jews, could think in terms of space (Gehenna or Hades/earth/heaven). Gehenna or heaven may be the future lot of individuals, but some may enter heaven or Gehenna at death, before the *eschaton*.[3]

Mark mentions Gehenna in one passage (9:43, 45, 47), Matthew more frequently, and Luke only once (12:5, but Hades, 16:23). We have already noted that in Matthew the Kingdom has a heavenly aspect.

There are clear traces in Luke of space eschatology. In the parable of the Rich Man and Lazarus (16:19–31), Abraham's bosom and Hades may be merely conventional, for the sake of the story, but there is also the story of the penitent bandit who asks to be remembered when Jesus comes into his kingdom and receives the answer "Today you will be with me in paradise" (23:42–43).

This type of thinking is not nearly so evident in Mark. One can think of the controversy with the Sadducees (Mark 12:18–27 = Matt 22:23–33 =

Kaiser, 1955) 55–91, but it was employed in criticism much earlier by H. B. Sharman, *Son of Man and Kingdom of God* (New York: Harper, 1943) 89.

[3] Cf. 4 Macc 7:19, 16:25, 17:5.

Luke 20:27–40), in which Abraham, Isaac and Jacob are spoken of as living. Luke makes the point even clearer, "for all live to him" (20:38). Heaven of course is where Jesus is seated before his return; this is suggested by the important quotation of Ps 110:1 (Mark 12:37) and by Mark 14:62 = Luke 22:69.

Mark

Mark begins his gospel with the preaching of John the Baptizer, Jesus' baptism, and his testing in the wilderness. It is not John who announces the Reign of God, but Jesus.

Most treatments of Jesus' message in Mark assume that the Reign of God is an entirely future event. This position has recently been challenged by Werner H. Kelber in his book, *The Kingdom in Mark*. If Kelber's thesis is correct, Mark has an understanding of the Reign of God which is significantly different from those of Matthew and Luke.

Kelber's thesis proceeds from his interpretation of 1:15, which can be summarized as follows; the time (the decisive moment) has fully arrived, and the Kingdom of God is present; repent and believe by means of the gospel. Thus Kelber takes ἤγγικεν as essentially equivalent to ἔφθασεν (Matt 12:28 = Luke 11:20). In some real sense the Kingdom has arrived in Jesus' activity and preaching; it is manifested in his teaching and in his conflict with the kingdom of evil and the old kingdom, the present order.[4] His conclusion is that the gospel heralds a new place, Galilee, and a new time.

The strength of Kelber's theory is that the Kingdom is the theme of the first of the three major collections of Jesus' teaching in Mark, and that in 9:1 Jesus promises that some of those with him will see it present in power. The complete advent of God's Reign will be when the Son of Man returns to Galilee.

It is however, curious that the phrase does not appear between 1:15 and Chap. 4, though in the meantime Mark refers several times to Jesus' preaching and teaching (1:21–22, 27, 38; 2:2 ["the word"], 13). In corresponding parts of Matthew and Luke, the Kingdom is mentioned more often, as it is throughout those gospels. Does Mark think it unnecessary to mention the Kingdom, even in passages where, as Kelber assumes, it is

---

[4] See, e.g., Kelber, *The Kingdom in Mark*, on the miracles in Chap. 1 (15–18) and the controversies in Chap. 2 and 3:1–6 (18–23). The mention of Satan's kingdom in 3:23–26 is another example of the collision of the two kingdoms.

in combat with evil, or is it simply that the phrase does not appear in the sources he is using?

Two parables in Mark 4 are explicitly Kingdom parables, the Seed Growing Secretly (4:26–29) and the Mustard-seed (4:30–32). Prior to these, in 4:11–12, Jesus speaks of the revelation and hiding of the secret of the Kingdom. These two verses have puzzled commentators perhaps more than any part of this gospel. What is the mystery? Is it partly disclosed in the interpretation of the Sower (4:13–20) and in the parables that follow? Many exegetes argue that in Mark's theology God has condemned "those outside" to blindness and deafness; but the purpose of a lamp is to give light, and nothing is hidden except to be revealed (4:21–22), so that other scholars hold that the outsiders fail to hear because they will not open their ears and minds. In this case Mark does not seriously disagree with the thought in Matt 13:13.

There is also a literary problem. Matt 13:11 and Luke 8:10 have the verb γνῶναι, as Mark does not; "to you it is given *to know*." Matthew teaches more than once that the disciples understand Jesus' nature and message (e.g., 14:33, 16:12) and in this he differs from Mark. γνῶναι is a "minor agreement" between Matthew and Luke. Joel Marcus explains this by the theory that all three evangelists knew the saying from oral tradition but Mark omitted the word because of his belief that the disciples did not fully understand the mystery until after the Resurrection. Thus in Mark they occupy an intermediate position. They have been granted the mystery which is withheld from the crowds and have some perception of Jesus' nature, but not as fully as the demons, who know him as the holy one of God (Mark 1:24) and Son of God (3:11, 5:7).[5]

After Caesarea Philippi references to the Reign of God appear more frequently, as do Son of Man sayings. The emphasis in Chaps. 9 and 10, as in the parallel passage in Matthew and Luke, is on conditions for entering the Reign of God, or inheriting it, or being excluded from it. "Kingdom of God" and "eternal life" are used interchangeably in the sayings on scandals (9:43–48; cf. Matt 18:8–9). Similarly, children are fit for God's Kingdom (10:14; cf. Matt 18:3), while in 10:17 the rich man asks what he must do to inherit eternal life. The ensuing discussion concerns the Kingdom of God (10:23–26), but in the second part of it those who have left families and lands are promised eternal life (10:30 = Matt 19:29).

[5] Joel Marcus, *The Mystery of the Kingdom of God* (Atlanta: Scholars Press, 1986) 84–86, 99.

In such places the Reign of God is something like Matthew's heavenly Kingdom.

James and John ask Jesus for places of honor in his "glory" (10:37), but in Matt 20:21 it is their mother who asks that they may have special rank "in your kingdom." Thus, whether Mark is editing Matthew or *vice versa*, the two evangelists are not consistent in the changes they make.

Both Matt 26:29 and Mark 14:25 contain Jesus' statement that he will not drink wine again until he drinks it in the Kingdom of God. Matthew's phrase, "kingdom of my Father," is in accord with his style and theology.

It must be said in favor of Kelber's thesis that Mark continues to remind his readers of the message of the Kingdom; thus when the scribe agrees with Jesus' summary of the law, he responds "You are not far from the Kingdom of God" (12:34, only in Mark). He states that Joseph of Arimathaea is one who expects the Kingdom of God (15:4 = Luke 23:51), but in Matt 27:57 Joseph is a disciple of Jesus.

Kelber, then, holds that Mark expects God's Reign to be established when Jesus is reunited with his disciples in Galilee. The Kingdom, however, remains partly a secret, for Mark speaks only of the coming of Jesus. Matthew pictures a meeting with the disciples in Galilee, but what occurs there is the establishment of Jesus' reign; the Son of Man has a kingdom distinct from that of the Father. Luke's conclusion is quite different; the resurrection and ascension are followed by the establishment of the church at Pentecost, and the return of Jesus is still in the future.

Conclusion

Reign of God sayings appear in the sources of all three synoptic gospels, whether one follows the GH or the 2DH, and in the underlying tradition they are separate from Son of Man sayings. Matthew appears to be secondary to Mark and Q for several reasons. It is likely that he is responsible for the phrase "Kingdom of the heavens," and that he conceives this realm as essentially heavenly; the coming of the Kingdom implies that God's will is to be done on earth as it is in heaven (6:9). His tendency to moralize the Beatitudes (5:6) fits with this. The Kingdom of the Father is distinct from that of the Son of Man (13:43, 26:29), and he is the only evangelist to introduce the Son of Man into a Kingdom saying (16:28).

The logion on the messianic banquet in Matt 8:11–12 appears to be added to the pericope of the Centurion of Capharnaum, and Luke 13:27–

29 seems to have it in a more natural context; it is, however, a self-contained saying.

It is curious that in Matthew John the Baptizer is the first to announce the Reign of God, but perhaps this is because he is identified with Elijah (11:14). The tradition appears to be uncertain whether John actually belongs to the Kingdom (11:11 = Luke 7:28). In Matt 12:28 Jesus casts out demons by the Spirit of God; in Luke 11:20 by the finger of God. If it is Luke who made the change he has introduced an allusion to Exod 8:19.

Of the three evangelists, it is Luke who is most likely to have introduced a mention of the Reign of God into sayings (e.g., 9:60, 18:29). Mark does not use the phrase between 1:15 and 4:11. Kelber's theory that the Kingdom is a theme found throughout Mark does not affect the issue between the GH and the 2DH, although it presumes the priority of Mark.

CHAPTER SIX

The Parables Discourse

The parables discourse (Mark 1:1–34) provides an important oppor-
tunity to test the GH and the 2DH, both with respect to the concept of the
Reign of God contained therein, and the editorial habits of the three
Synoptic evangelists.

One should begin with an overview of Matt 13:1–52, which follows
the narrative portion (11:2–12:50) of what we have called the Old and the
New.

Jesus is seated in a boat near the shore, and the crowd is on the land.
The parable of the Sower follows (13:3–9), the climax of which is that the
good seed falls on soil that produces hundredfold, sixtyfold, and thirtyfold. The disciples approach Jesus and ask why he speaks in parables; his
answer is that it is because the crowd looks and looks and does not understand. Jesus then quotes Isa 6:9–10 using Matthew's characteristic
formula (13:10–15). But blessed are the eyes of the disciples, for they see
what prophets and righteous men had not seen (13:16–17). The parable is
then explained as an allegory of the seed (13:18–23).

Next come three parables , the Weeds (13:24–30), the Mustard-seed
(13:31–32), and the Yeast (13:33). The first part of the discourse concludes
with another formula quotation from "the prophet" (Ps 78:2; Matt 13:35).
As in most of Matthew's formula citations, this is an independent translation, agreeing only in part with the LXX.

Jesus now leaves the crowd and goes into "the house" (his house?
13:36). Here in private he explains the allegory of the Weeds[1] and gives
three other parables, the Hid Treasure, the Pearl, and the Seine (13:44–
50). The last of these is given an interpretation. The section concludes

---

[1] J. D. Kingsbury, *The Parables of Jesus in Matthew 13* (Richmond: John Know Press,
1969) 22–91.

with the little picture of the scribe who has been made a disciple to the Kingdom of the heavens (13:51-52). Thus Matthew indicates that the second half of the discourse applies especially to the intimate disciples.

Matthew's characteristic expressions appear several times in 13:1–52, e.g., καὶ προσελθόντες . . .αὐτῷ (v. 10, cf. v. 36), ἄλλην παραβολήν (vv. 24, 31), ἐκεῖ ἔσται ὁ κλαυθμὸς κτλ. (vv. 42, 50), and ναί (v. 51).

Luke's discourse is much shorter (8:4–12). Whether his source is Matthew or Mark, he abbreviates. The contrast between the outsiders and the disciples who understand the mystery (8:9–10) and the explanation of the Sower (8:10–15) are made as brief as possible, and there is only the one parable. The Mustard-seed and the Yeast appear in a different context (13:18–21), and the discourse concludes with a group of sayings found in some form in Matt 5:15 (the lamp); 10:26 ([more] will be given, etc.). The effect of this is that in Luke the disciples know the mystery, which will come completely to light, and they are to be alert in listening. The visit of the family to Jesus comes after this (8:19–21).

Mark is the middle term here. The GH would assume that Mark has used parts of Matthew and, toward the end, parts of Luke. But in that case he has produced a discourse with a very different effect, and his composition needs to be explained. If he has drawn the picture of Jesus in the boat from Matt 13:1–2, he has made the statement (clumsy or vivid) that Jesus "sat in the sea," and he carefully prepared for this by the ordering of the boat in 3:9.

In none of the three gospels is the parable of the Sower (4:3–9) explicitly a parable of the Kingdom, except that in the interpretation in Matt 13:19 the seed is equated with the message of the Kingdom. It has therefore been suggested that Mark uses this as a typical parable to which he appends an interpretation as an example of how parables should be understood. Yet Mark may think of the Sower as a parable of the Kingdom, because in 4:10–11 Jesus says to "those around him with the Twelve. . .'To you has been given the secret of the Reign of God, but to those outside everything becomes parables'" (here the word seems to mean "dark sayings, riddles"). Thus, if the Sower was intended to be a typical parable, this must have been so in the source underlying Mark or Matthew. In any case, Mark seems to teach that a parable must be allegorized, and in this respect all three evangelists disagree with those modern interpreters who hold that normally a parable is not an allegory; either it has a single point or it is open-ended.[2]

If one is to suppose that in 4:10-12 Mark is rewriting Matthew, (1) he changes προσελθόντες to say that Jesus gave this instruction in private, (2) he follows Luke (8:18) in postponing Matt 13:13b to later in the discourse (Mark 4:25), (3) omits the formula citation, Matt 13:14–15, but picks up the end of the quotation from Isaiah, using not the LXX as Matthew does, but an independent translation.[3] Here the 2DH seems a simpler solution, though one has to recognize that 4:10 is in Mark's style and that Matt 13:11 and Luke 8:10 have γνῶναι τὰ μυστήρια while Mark does not have γνῶναι and writes the singular τὸ μυστήριον. One might say that Mark includes 4:11–12 because it is in his tradition, even though it fits with difficulty into his evaluation of the disciples.[4]

One must call attention to the fact that Jesus' congratulation to the disciples for seeing and hearing in Matt 13:16–17 is lacking in Mark. Luke includes this in a similar form in Jesus' address to "the disciples" after the Seventy-two have returned (10:23–24). If this is not a Q passage, the GH would have to suppose that Luke has made up 10:1–24 out of various passages in Matthew, postponing this logion to Chapter 10, or that he has a separate source for parts of the chapter. In this case, Mark follows Luke in omitting the logion in his Chap. 4; he does not, of course, pick it up from Luke's Central Section, because in any case it contradicts his criticism of the disciples. Supporters of the 2DH, however, see Matthew's inclusion of 13:16–17 as one more indication, to be added to several others, that Matthew softens the negative portrait of the Twelve.[5]

---

[2] A. Jülicher's contention that normally a parable expresses a single idea or principle dominated gospel study for a long time. For parables as multivalent, see, e.g., J.D. Crossan, *In Parables* (New York: Harper & Row, 1985) 8–15; N. Perrin, *Jesus and the Language of the Kingdom* (Philadelphia: Fortress, 1980) 30–32, 133–39, 157–58, 201–203.

[3] Curiously, Matthew here agrees with Acts 28:26–27; cf. S. E. Johnson, "The Biblical Quotations in Matthew," *HTR* 36 (1943) 137–38.

[4] See p. 82 above and note 5 to Chap. 5.

[5] C. M. Tuckett, *The Revival of the Griesbach Hypothesis: An Analysis and Appraisal* (Cambridge: Cambridge University Press, 1985) 90–93, discusses Matt 13:16–17 = Luke 10:23–24 in great detail. He remarks: "According to Farmer's theory, Mark must have switched at this point to following Luke as his main source; but then, in the first two logia, he must have omitted very carefully all those small details which bring Luke's version closer to Matthew. . . Far from reproducing the 'concurrent testimony' of his sources, Mark seems carefully to have avoided doing so at this point." Tuckett thinks that at Mark 4:12 the evangelist had independent versions of the sayings and did not depend upon Q or Luke.

Mark 4:21–25 seems to contradict the idea that the parables deliberately conceal the message; the purpose of a lamp is to be put on the lampstand. Mark, however, warns that one must have ears to hear; the wise become wiser and the stupid more obtuse. If one supposes that Mark is following Luke at this point, it is necessary to say that Luke has borrowed and rewritten the substance of Matt 5:15; 10:26 and 13:12, and that Mark (4:24) has inserted a saying from Matt 7:2. This seems most unlikely.

The parable of the Self-Growing Seed (or the Patient Farmer) is found only in Mark 4:26–29. It proclaims that the Reign of God, hidden and secret now, will come to complete fulfillment; at the end there is a brief quotation from Joel 4:13, which originally spoke of judgment and is so used in Rev 14:18. It is curious that some of the words used in this parable appear also in the parable of the Weeds, which appears in Matt 13:24–30 in the same relative position. It seems too much to believe that Mark has taken a few words from Matthew and built up this amazing parable; a better solution is that Mark has a separate source. The *Gospel of Thomas* has forms both of Mark's parable (21b) and Matthew's (57).[6]

The parable of the Mustard-seed has a form similar to that of the preceding one. The Reign of God is inevitable and will be great. The contrast, however, is between the small and the great, and in place of a suggestion of Judgment the Kingdom is a shelter for the birds of the sky.

Matt 13:31–32 and Luke 13:18–19 present the parable in different forms. Matthew's introduction is a simple comparison, but in the other gospels there is something like a rabbinic formula, "A parable. To what is the matter like? It is like. . ." Matthew and Luke say that the Kingdom grows into a tree and the birds roost in its branches, but while Matthew says that "a man sowed it in his field," in Luke "a man cast it into his garden." Mark seemingly does not think of a tree, rather it is the greatest of all shrubs, and the birds nest under its shade; yet Ezek 17:23, quoted here, originally referred to a cedar; cf. also Dan 4:12, 21.

When the three gospels are compared, the GH would demand that Mark has conflated the parables in Matthew and Luke, has produced a more wordy and colloquial introduction, used ἀναβαίνει καὶ γίνεται in place of forms of αὐξάνω and avoided the question of a field or a garden. Luke's parable is practically a Mark-free version of the parable in

---

6 Cf. Crossan, *In Parables*, 85. Montefiore, however, argued that Thomas' form of the Weeds parable is an abbreviation of Matthew (H. Montefiore and H. E. W. Turner, *Thomas and the Evangelists* [Naperville, Ill: Allenson, 1962] 51–52.)

Matthew! The alternative hypothesis is that Mark and Luke had separate forms of the parable, and that it is Matthew who has done the conflating. The same phenomenon of Matthew as the middle term between Mark and Luke (or Q) can be observed elsewhere.[7]

Whatever view of synoptic relationships is adopted, Mark has decided that the Seed parables are sufficient for his purpose, to proclaim that God's Reign is near and inevitable. These also suggest that its coming will involve God's judgment and a shelter for his people.

In a recent book, John Donahue studies the corpus of parables in the Synoptics and the way in which each of the three gospels is, taken as a whole, a "parable." He observes that Matthew integrates ethics and eschatology in his characteristic fashion. Luke retains the eschatology in his sources but shifts attention away from the *eschaton* to "today" (e.g., 13:32; 19:5, 9). In contrast, Mark's gospel is characterized by concrete realism, paradox and wonder, and an open-ended quality.[8]

When one asks how these traits appear in the parables, it is easy to see that Matthew regularly relates eschatology to ethics (e.g., Matt 13:41–43, 47–50). In rewriting Mark 4, Luke includes only the Sower and its interpretation; the Mustard-seed and the Yeast appear at 13:18–21 following the healing of the crippled woman (13:10–17). The parables of Luke 15 and some others peculiar to this evangelist (16:1–8, 18:10–14) are non-eschatological. Others are certainly eschatological (12:35–46, 18:1–8), but in these cases the emphasis is on the behavior and attitudes of people here and now.

Donahue's remarks on Mark apply best to the Seed parables and to the Doorkeeper (13:33–35), but the parallels to these in Matthew and

---

[7] Tuckett, *Griesbach Hypothesis*, 78–85, analyzes the peculiarities of the Sower thoroughly, and concludes that there are two independent versions, Marcan and Lucan (Q); here Mark is not using Q. "Mark has systematically avoided everything common to Matthew and Luke. . . Mark appears to have taken an intense dislike to Luke" (80). Advocates of the GH regard an overlap of sources as a desperate expedient; yet Farmer admits parallel sources for the parables of the Lost Sheep and the Talents or Pounds (*The Synoptic Problem: A Critical Analysis* [New York: Macmillan, 1964] 77). Another approach can be seen in the article by F. Gerald Downing, "Compositional Conventions and the Synoptic Problem," *JBL* 107 (1988) 69–85. Here he develops an argument used in his previous article, "Towards the Rehabilitation of 'Q'" *NTS* 11 (1965) 169–81, by a study of sources used by Josephus, Plutarch and others. This affects the baptism and temptation narratives (Mark 1:9–13 and parallels), the various mission charges, and the Synoptic apocalypse. He concludes that the 2DH fits best the compositional methods of Matthew and Luke and that they are using Mark and Q much as Hellenistic writers used their sources.

[8] J. R. Donahue, *The Gospel in Parable* (Philadelphia: Fortress, 1988) 194–216.

Luke retain the concreteness and paradox that one finds in Mark. The parables themselves are open-ended, but even Mark blunts this by adding interpretations (4:14–20; 13:32–33, 37). Nevertheless, when Donahue's discussion is reviewed in the light of the GH and 2DH, Mark appears to be independent of the other two gospels; his treatment of the parables does not derive from Matthew or Luke.

CHAPTER SEVEN

Christology

Matthew

There is a basic unity in the Christologies of the Synoptics, but each of the evangelists has his characteristic understanding of the Christ of faith. This is to be seen in the way in which they use the various titles—Messiah, Son of God, Son of Man, Lord, and so on—but especially in their narratives of Jesus' ministry and the methods by which they edit his sayings and place them in context.

It is best to begin with Matthew, for this gospel has a highly developed and integrated Christology, and the characteristics of Luke and Mark will stand out more clearly if they are discussed afterward. Matthew writes for a Christian community and can presuppose that his readers approximately share his faith. The actors in the drama, however, have to learn this, and it is instructive to see how the evangelist pictures the disclosure of Jesus' nature to the crowds, who are a symbol of potential or actual converts, and especially to the "disciples," who typify the Church's future leaders.

Messiah and Son of God

In the first few chapters the readers learn at once, if they do not already know it, that Jesus is the Messiah as the legal descendant of David. The magi come looking for a child who is to be born king of the Jews. The context of the quotation referring to Galilee in 4:15–16 (Isa 8:23–9:1) is in a messianic passage; the one who is to bring the great light is a descendant of David. Later the Canaanite woman (15:22) and the two blind men (20:29–34) address Jesus as Lord, Son of David. Jesus will promise

Peter the keys, and this is to make him the steward in a royal household (Isa 22:22).[1]

As Son of God, the gospel of Matthew portrays Jesus with divine traits. His disciples approach him as though he were a king (Matthew uses προσέρχομαι in a characteristic way) and they offer him obeisance or worship (προσκυνέω, e.g., in 14:38; after the resurrection, 28:9, 17). People who have faith in him address him as Lord (8:2, 6; 14:28, 30), especially in a cry for help (15:21, 20:51).[2]

Immediately after his baptism, in the temptation story, the devil addresses Jesus as Son of God (4:1–11 = Luke 4:1–13). Here Jesus shows his loyalty and perfect knowledge of the will of God by his correct interpretation of Scripture. I have previously mentioned the theory that there is an aretalogy lying behind Mark in which Jesus is portrayed as a divine man or hero, and it is alleged that Luke is especially given to this trait. But the temptation pericope is a type of story found in many religious literatures in which such a hero is tested, often at the outset of his ministry. In other parts of Matthew the divine traits are evident as Jesus heals, exorcises demons, stills the storm, feeds the multitudes, and walks on the water. There is actually rather little difference between the gospels as regards the divine man tradition.

Matthew gives no indication that when the four fishermen follow Jesus (4:18–22) they know of his divine nature. He now heals and teaches in the synagogue and proclaims the Good News of the Kingdom (4:23–25). Presumably the four fishermen are among the disciples who hear the Sermon on the Mount. As he teaches about the Kingdom and its righteousness, they learn the truth first suggested in the temptation story that Jesus' knowledge of God's will is in harmony with Scripture but goes beyond its letter, so that he can give authoritative interpretation of it (e.g., 5:21–48).[3] Jesus speaks frequently of "my Father" and also of "your father," but only in the Lord's Prayer of "our Father." Other human beings become children of God when they imitate the Father (5:45, 48). But this does no more than to hint at Jesus' unique sonship. It is only in the pericope 7:21–27 that Jesus is Lord and that there will be those who cast out demons in his name.

---

[1] S. E. Johnson, "The Davidic-Royal Motif in the Gospels," *JBL* 87 (1968) 140-43; J. D. Kingsbury, "The Title 'Son of David' in Matthew's Gospel," *JBL* 95 (1976) 591–602.

[2] J. D. Kingsbury, *Jesus Christ in Matthew, Mark, and Luke* (Philadelphia: Fortress, 1981) 74–76.

[3] Kingsbury, *Jesus Christ*, 76.

Servant of the Lord and Son of Man

Other aspects of Jesus' person and work begin to appear in 8:1–9:35. Here his activity furnishes the disciples with a pattern of what they must do if they follow him. This section sets the stage for his appointment of the Twelve and directions for their mission (9:36–10:42). Healing and exorcism are prominent in these chapters, and now Jesus is identified with the Servant of the Lord in the songs of Second Isaiah. The emphasis, however, is not on the future suffering of Jesus; rather "He himself took our sicknesses and carried (away) our diseases" (8:17; Isa 53:4.)[4]

It is also in Chapter 8 that Jesus first refers to himself as Son of Man. When a certain scribe offers to follow him, he replies that the Son of Man has nowhere to lay his head (8:20). In the story of the paralytic, Jesus announces that the Son of Man has authority on earth to forgive sins (9:6). This is also a self-designation, and Matthew evidently assumes that the crowds understood it so (Son of Man = a man, this man), for they glorified God, who had given such authority to human beings (9:8). To Matthew's readers the phrase would have meant much more.

As every exegete recognizes, the Son of Man sayings in the gospels exhibit great variety. Later I shall show that there is no pattern in these logia in Matthew prior to the Caesarea Philippi pericope.

There are other features in Matt 8–9 that may be due merely to the evangelist's use of sources, but since these chapters are carefully constructed to lead to the call of the Twelve, Matthew may use these features to suggest that the disciples are gradually learning from Jesus' words and deeds. When there is a storm on the lake they address him as κύριε (8:25) and afterward ask, "What sort of person is this, that the winds and the sea obey him?" (8:27). They also hear the Gadarene demoniacs address Jesus as Son of God (8:29) and hear the enigmatic prophecy that the bridegroom will be taken away (9:15).

Further Disclosures

Jesus tells that Twelve in the mission charge that the Son of Man will come before they have gone through all the cities of Israel (10:23), that acceptance by God depends upon confessing Jesus openly (10:32–33),

---

[4] The details in the Passion Narrative which echo Isa 52:13–53:12 and 50:6 (Matt 26:24, 53, 67; 27:12, 14, 30, 38) are practically all found in Mark and were probably part of the traditional story, whether Matthew or Mark is the earlier gospel. Matthew does not call attention to the biblical passages except that in 26:24 Jesus speaks of the fulfillment of Scripture.

and finally that anyone who receives Jesus receives the One who sent him (10:40).

Then in 11:25–30 Jesus reveals his unique sonship and calls on his hearers to accept his easy yoke, but Matthew says nothing about the audience. The evangelist is apparently not interested in whether or not this has been taught to the disciples.

The next disclosure comes when some scribes and Pharisees ask Jesus for a sign. In Matthew's form of this pericope (12:38–42; cf. Luke 11:29–32), the sign of Jonah is Jesus' death and resurrection; the Son of Man will be in the heart of the earth three days and three nights.

The dignity of the Son of Man is further explained in two parables, the Weeds (13:24–30) and the Seine (13:47–50). The Son of Man has a kingdom which will be superseded by the Kingdom of the Father (13:41–43; cf. the parable of the Last Judgment, 25:31–46).

After the Feeding of the Five Thousand, Jesus walks on the waters ("I am," 14:22–27). Peter now attempts to come to him on the waters, but fails and is rescued (14:28–32); this is a lesson in faith and Matthew uses his characteristic word ὀλιγόπιστε. The disciples in the boat now make a formal confession of faith, "Truly you are Son of God" (14:33). As in 13:16–17, the disciples do indeed understand.

Caesarea Philippi

Matthew's Christology, and the disciples' formal acknowledgement of Jesus, is substantially complete in the scene at Caesarea Philippi (16:13–28 = Mark 8:27–9:1 = Luke 9:18–27).

The pericope is a turning point in the gospels of Matthew and Mark, less obviously so in Luke. From this point on the story points toward the Passion. It is here that Peter makes his full Christological confession: "You are the Messiah, the Son of the living God" (16:16) and Jesus answers, "Blessed are you, Simon Barjona, because flesh and blood has not revealed it to you, but my Father who is in the heavens" (16:17). One may contrast this with Mark 8:27–33, where Jesus bids the disciples to be silent and goes on to speak of the suffering of the Son of Man (cf. also Luke 9:13–22). Matthew, like Mark, records Peter's rejection of the thought that Jesus must suffer (16:22–23), but this comes only after the blessing on Peter, who has correctly discerned part of the mystery.[5]

---

5 It may be argued that Matthew is more severe than Mark because he calls Peter a σκάνδαλον (16:23), but this noun, usually in the plural, is a favorite with Matthew; he also uses the verb σκανδαλίζω more frequently than the other evangelists.

One may speak of a "messianic secret" in Mark, but in Matthew it is a secret withheld from the outsiders, not the disciples. In Matthew the Caesarea Philippi pericope is a climax and summary of what has gone before, not a new revelation. As contrasted with Mark, there is no pattern in the Son of Man sayings up to this point. Here the first explicit Passion predictions begin, as in the parallel section of Mark, but even this has been anticipated by the statement that when the disciples are persecuted it is no more than that which Jesus suffered (10:24–25) and especially by the veiled reference to Jesus' death and resurrection in the Sign of Jonah saying (12:40).

The Son of Man in Matthew

At this point it may be helpful to tabulate the previous occurrences of "Son of Man" in Matthew.

It has long been recognized that there are three basic types of Son of Man sayings in the Synoptics: (a) eschatological logia in which the Son of Man is to come in the future; (b) non-eschatological ones in which Jesus uses the term as a self-designation; and (c) sayings predicting that the Son of Man will suffer, die, and rise again.[6]

The sayings prior to Caesarea Philippi are as follows:

8:20–21 (=Luke 9:58). The Son of Man has no place to lay his head.

9:6–7 (=Mark 2:10=Luke 5:24). He has authority on earth to forgive sins.

10:23. The disciples will not have finished going through the cities of Israel before he comes.

11:16–19 (=Luke 7:31–35). He came eating and drinking and was criticized as a wine-drinker and a friend of tax collectors and sinners.

12:8 (=Mark 2:28=Luke 6:5). He is Lord of the sabbath.

12:32 (=Luke 12:10). A word against the Son of Man can be forgiven, but not a word against the Holy Spirit.

12:38–42 (cf. Luke 11:29–32). As Jonah was in the belly of the whale, so the Son of Man will be in the heart of the earth.

---

6 The literature is immense and continually growing. Lake analyzed the three types of sayings in K. Lake and F. J. Foakes Jackson, *The Beginnings of Christianity. I. The Acts of the Apostles* (London: Macmillan, 1920) I. 368–84. See the bibliographies in articles by S. E. Johnson and N. Perrin, "Son of Man," in *IDB* 4. 413–20; *IDB* Suppl 633–35.

13:37–43, 47–50. The Son of Man sows good seed; he has a kingdom out of which he will collect scandals, etc.

Most of the above instances are self-identification (Son of Man = I myself). The two which picture Jesus as the homeless and rejected prophet are non-eschatological. So probably are 9:6 and 12:8, which are the only Son of Man sayings to appear in Mark prior to Peter's confession, and they are distinctive because they claim authority for Jesus. 12:32 may belong here but only because of its context in the Beelzebul controversy.[7] At the same time this saying has a reference to the future judgment.

The Sign of Jonah pericope is also peculiar in that it involves the judgment. The men of Nineveh and the Queen of the South will be witnesses against the present generation. Here the Son of Man saying is apparently a self-designation, as it is in Luke 11:30, but Matthew understands the sign of Jonah as a type of the three days after Jesus' death. In Luke the sign is his preaching, which brings repentance, and this fits better with the rest of the pericope which makes essentially the same point as a saying in Mark 8:11–12; no sign will be given this generation except the signs that everyone should recognize (cf. Luke 16:19–31 for the example of a similar idea). The phenomenon in Matt 12:40 is a difficulty for the GH; it is most likely that Matthew has edited a pericope in Q.[8]

Another saying in the mission discourse (10:23) predicts the coming of the Son of Man. The interpretation of the parable of the Weeds refers to his kingdom and implies his activity as judge. There is therefore no pattern in Matthew's use of the title up to 16:13.

After 16:13 (in the Caesarea Philippi section) there are twelve instances in which Matthew uses the phrase, to which there are parallels in Mark (Matt 16:23, 28; 17:9, 12, 22; 20:18, 28: 24:30; 26:24 (bis), 45, 64). From 8:27 on, these are the only occurrences of Son of Man in Mark, with the exception of 8:31.

---

[7] In Luke 12:8 Jesus does not explicitly identify himself as Son of Man ("whoever acknowledges me, the Son of Man will acknowledge him"), whereas the parallel, Matt 10:32, reads "I will acknowledge."

[8] Cf. C. H. Talbert and E. V. McKnight, "Can the Griesbach Hypotheses be Falsified?" *JBL* 91 (1972) 361–64. McKnight argues that Matt 12:40 is secondary because (1) is it more specific, a criterion that Farmer later withdrew, (2) it interrupts the course of thought or symmetry or plan in Luke (Burton's criterion), (3) it inserts matter for which motivation is clear in the light of the author's general aim, while no motive can be discovered for its insertion by the other author if he had it in his source (Burton), and (4) it adds τοῦ προφήτου, a word often used by Matthew.

The revelation of Jesus' nature, and the understanding of the disciples, therefore, come to a climax in the Caesarea Philippi scene and the Transfiguration. Peter's confession is full and explicit (16:16). Jesus predicts the suffering of the Son of Man (16:21) and his coming to judge; in their lifetime some of the disciples will see him coming to judge; in their lifetime some of the disciples will see him coming in his kingdom (16:27–28).[9] Finally, the Transfiguration gives them a glimpse of his hidden nature and his future glory.

This review of Matthew's Christology shows that the fundamental concept is that Jesus is Son of God. Perhaps the most important datum is the way in which the narrative portrays him as a divine person.[10] His humanity is not denied: although he resists temptation he must undergo it, and he will suffer and die. The humanity of the disciples is related to his own; at least morally and spiritually they can become children of God also (5:44–45). The other titles, Messiah, son of David, Son of Man, Lord and Servant of God, are aspects of this integrated Christology, and interpret what it means to be God's Son.

Luke

The Christology of Luke is in many ways parallel to that of Matthew. For example, Luke shows that from the moment of his conception Jesus is Messiah, Son of God, and Savior; yet he develops this in his characteristic way.

The annunciation to Mary is expressed in the purest royal-messianic terms (1:29–31). Even "son of the Most High" does not go beyond 2 Sam 7:14; Pss 2:7, 89:26. The Canticles, 1:47–55, 68–79, are reminiscent of the canonical Psalms and the Psalms of Solomon and they reinforce the messianic theme. Peter's confession is that Jesus is "the Messiah of God."

But, as in Matthew, Jesus is Son of God in a more transcendent sense. Gabriel replies, in answer to Mary's question, that the Holy Spirit will come upon her and that it is God's Son who will be born (1:35). This is another aspect of sonship, but it is still an antitype of wondrous births related in the OT (e.g., Judg 13:3).

It is an interesting question whether the apparent development of Christology in Luke's story is due to the nature of his sources or reflects a decided sensitivity to historical perspective, so that the mystery of Jesus' being is progressively revealed. In any case, the meaning of Jesus' son-

---

9 Cf. Talbert and McKnight, "Griesbach Hypothesis," 344–53.
10 Kingsbury, *Jesus Christ*, 75–76.

ship comes out more clearly when in the Temple he speaks of his Father's house (2:49). Later the voice from heaven proclaims a special kind of sonship (3:22). At the same time, the genealogy, traced as in Matthew through Joseph, gives a line of descent from Adam, the Son of God (3:23–38). This can be read as expressing Jesus' solidarity with all humanity, and thus legitimizing the mission to Gentiles and linking his birth to God's purpose in creation.

The emphasis on Jesus' humanity fits with the many passages in Luke that exhibit his human traits and particularly sympathy with others, e.g., the story of the sinful woman (7:36–50) and the healing miracles in 13:10–16 and 14:1–6. This aspect of Jesus, which appears here and there in other gospels, must be partly the basis for the Church's later doctrine of the two natures of Christ. Although Luke finds such materials in his sources, he may use them deliberately. As my colleague William Countryman has remarked in conversation, the problem faced by the early Church from the beginning was not Jesus' divinity, which most Gentile Christians accepted, but his humanity.

More than in the other gospels Jesus is said to be at prayer (3:21, 6:12, 8:29, 11:1), and some of these instances are due to Luke's editing. Does the evangelist think of this as the natural impulse of a religious man, or is it that a divine man is often in conversation with his Father?

On one occasion Jesus disdains being a judge or a divider (12:14; cf. Exod 2:14). In his dialogue with Martha and Mary he is playful (10:38–42), but so are the philosophers.

The passages emphasizing Jesus' humanity strike a balance with other places where Jesus has the austere or remote bearing of a divine person. One aspect of his humanity is that he is a prophet. He is hailed as such when he raises the young man of Nain (7:16) and here there is a reminiscence of Elijah or Elisha. He is especially a prophet like Moses; his exorcisms are by the finger of God (11:20; cf. Exod 8:19). In Philo, of course, Moses is a semi-divine figure, and his miracles can be considered part of a θεῖος ἀνήρ portrayal. A θεῖος ἀνήρ is a benefactor and he does not lose his humanity during his earthly life.

In the same Lucan material, Jesus sometimes speaks in exultation and triumph, as in 10:17–20, when the Seventy-two return. Taken with 10:21–22 (=Matt 11:25–26), this is most impressive. He has come to cast fire on the earth (12:49–50, partly paralleled in Matt 10:34–36; cf. also *Gos. Thom.* 10, 16). Yet the element of human pathos comes in when Jesus is presented as a rejected prophet (7:31–35 = Matt 11:16–19; 9:58 = Matt 8:20). It is only in Jerusalem that a prophet can perish (13:31–33).

Many of Jesus' teachings are prophetic in nature, related to the Reign
of God and his mission to seek and save the lost, but he also appears as a
teacher within the community, arguing as a Jew among Jews, as in the
miracles of 13:10–16 and 14:1–6 mentioned above, and especially in many
of the parables, whose authority rest solely on the teaching embodied in
them. These traits are shared to some degree with the other gospels, but
Luke's choice of materials discloses his special interest in Jesus as teacher
of repentance, forgiveness, humility, compassion, holy poverty, and
prayer.

Still another aspect of Jesus' humanity appears when, in his visit to
the Temple at the age of twelve, he is called παῖς. In this context the word
most naturally means "boy," but Luke's use of it is significant because it
can also mean "servant," and is used in preaching and prayer to refer to
Jesus (Acts 3:13, 26; 4:25, 27, 30). Luke may have the Servant of Yahweh
in Isa 52:13–53:12 in mind when the risen Christ speaks of "Moses and all
the prophets" in teaching that the Messiah must suffer and enter into his
glory (Luke 24:25–27; cf. 24:46). Luke omits the pericope containing Matt
20:28 = Mark 10:45, λύτρον. Jesus goes to the Cross in obedience and because his death was predetermined. This is not proclaimed as a saving
act.[11] An examination of Luke's treatment of possible references to the
Servant Songs in Second Isaiah tends to confirm this.[12]

Jesus is a Savior who is Messiah the Lord (2:11). He liberates human
beings through his exorcisms and the many healings that Luke records
(see especially 13:16, 14:5, cf. 4:16–21 and Acts 10:38). By forgiveness he
also frees human beings from the old life of sin (e.g., Zacchaeus, 19:9)

---

[11] Luke of course does believe that Jesus gave his life for others. This is implied in
the words at the Last Supper, even if the longer text of Luke 22:17–24 is not accepted.
Yet the evangelist presents Jesus' death somewhat as a martyrdom, like that of the
holy people of the Maccabaean period.

[12] Luke 22:22 changes the wording of Matt 26:24 = Mark 14:21 to read "the Son of
Man goes as it has been determined," and in the pericope of the two swords Jesus
quotes from Isa 53:12, "and he was reckoned with the lawless" (22:37; cf. also 23:32).
The apparent parallels to Isa 53:7 ("he opened not his mouth") (Matt 26:63; 27:12, 14 =
Mark 14:61; 15:5) are lacking in Luke, and Jesus is silent only when interrogated by
Herod Antipas (Luke 23:9). If Luke is dependent on Matt 26:67 or Mark 14:65, the
evangelist does not seem conscious of an allusion to Isa 50:6, for he does not mention
the spitting. Jesus is led away (23:26, as in Matt 27:31; cf. Mark 15:18, 22), but an echo
is not certain here. Other quotations and possible references to the Servant Songs in
Luke-Acts do not concern the Passion (Jesus is a light to the Gentiles, Luke 2:32; Acts
13:47: cf. Isa 49:6) except in the long quotation in Acts 8:32–33 which is explained as
referring to Jesus, but nothing is made of salvation through the Cross.

and from many restrictions of the oral law (11:37–46). F. W. Danker has called special attention to the theme of liberation in Luke.[13]

The concept of Jesus as savior and benefactor fits with ideas of the Hellenistic cult-hero. So does the frequent use of κύριε only by those who have at least the beginnings of faith; by Peter (5:8, 12:41, 22:33), by James and John (9:54, at the Samaritan village), by the disciples (10:17, 11:1, 22:38), by Martha (10:40), the centurion of Capharnaum (7:6), and the blind beggar (18:41).[14] κύριος can have a wide range of reference, from "Sir" to persons of rank and gods, but Luke is unusual among the evangelists in his use of κύριος as a designation of Jesus (7:13, 19; 10:1, 39, 41; 17:5–6; 18:6; 22:61; 24:3 in some MSS, 34; perhaps in 16:8; cf. also 19:31, 34). Luke would therefore give his readers the impression that Jesus' rank is comparable to that of Yahweh; the LXX regularly translates the divine name as κύριος.

Luke's use of the title Son of Man is similar to that of Matthew prior to the passage Luke 17:22–37. The first occurrences, 5:24 and 6:5, correspond to the parallels in Mark and Matthew. It occurs in the Sermon in the fourth of the Beatitudes (6:22, ". . .cast out your name as evil for the sake of the Son of Man"). This appears to be a self-designation but it may have also a reference of the future coming of the Son of Man, and it is probably due to Luke's editing; cf. the conclusion of the eschatological discourse 21:36, "and to stand in the presence of the Son of Man."

Two other self-designations are in 7:34 (= Matt 11:19) and 9:58 (= Matt 8:20). In the Jonah pericope, the Son of Man, like Jonah, will be a sign to his generation (11:30). This self-designation probably looks to the future, because of the context (11:31–32). A third states that the Son of Man is come to seek and save the lost (19:10).

We have already mentioned 12:8, "whoever acknowledges [Jesus], the Son of Man will acknowledge him" (there is no Son of Man in the parallel Matt 10:32); and 12:10 (= Matt 12:32), a word against the Son of Man will be forgiven. These refer to the future judgment.

The Son of Man sayings in 17:22, 24, 30; 21:27, 36 are likewise eschatological. 17:24 has a parallel in Matt 24:27 (which mentions the

---

13 F. W. Danker, *Luke* (Philadelphia: Fortress, 1976) 6–17. The question of Luke's attitude to Torah and the Pharisees is complicated and will be discussed later.

14 The disciples also address Jesus as ἐπιστάτα, a term that implies his authority (8:24, 45; 9:33, 49), otherwise only the lepers do so (17:13). Outsiders, whether friendly or not, say διδάσκαλε (9:38; 10:25; 11:45; 12:13; 18:18, 20–21, 28), the disciples only once (21:7); they speak of him as ὁ διδάσκαλος in 22:11; cf. Mark 11:3 and Matt 21:3, ὁ κύριος.

Parousia), and 21:27 is parallel to Matt 24:20 and Mark 13:26. The saying which concludes the parable of the Unjust Judge, "Nevertheless, when the Son of Man comes, will he find faith on the earth?" (18:8) is probably Luke's addition.

The three Passion predictions (9:22, 44; 18:31–33) appear in passages that have parallels in Matthew and Mark. Luke's use of this tradition is, however, interesting. At the Last Supper, Jesus says that the Son of Man goes, as it has been determined (22:21). In 24:7, after the Resurrection, the two men in white remind the women of Jesus' prediction that the Son of Man must be crucified and rise again. A similar saying of Jesus to the disciples at Emmaus speaks of the Messiah (24:26) and the message is similar when he addresses the Eleven (24:46). Thus Luke integrates the Servant of Yahweh, the Messiah, and the Son of Man.

As in Matthew, there is no single pattern in the Son of Man sayings in Luke. It is essentially Jesus' self-designation which can have various references. The concept of Jesus as Son of God continues to play a part to the end (e.g., 22:29, 42; 23:34, 46), but the centurion does not use this phrase (23:47). Luke uses all the titles as aspects of the Messiah of God.

Mark: Son of God

When study of the Christologies of the Synoptic gospels is approached from the point of view of the 2DH, Matthew and Luke appear to reflect a development beyond Mark. If, however, the GH is adopted as a working hypothesis, a different picture emerges which calls for explanation.

Mark's first message to his readers is that Jesus is Son of God (1:1, 11), and the gospel is framed by these verses and the confession of the centurion in 15:39.[15]

The title that sums up Mark's Christology appears to be "Son of God." Perhaps it can be said that other titles, and indeed the gospel story as a whole, disclose aspects of this basic faith.

The demons know this truth and address Jesus as Son of God (3:11) and Son of the Most High (5:7 = Luke 8:28; cf. Matt 8:7, "Son of God"). "The holy one of God" (1:24 = Luke 4:34) may mean much the same thing. In one of the summaries of healings, Mark says, "he did not permit the demons to speak, because they knew him" (1:34); Luke 4:41, "knew

---

[15] υἱοῦ θεοῦ in 1:1 is omitted by a few important authorities, but it should be read here because of its otherwise good attestation and the fact that it fits with Mark's Christology elsewhere.

him to be the Messiah." It is Mark who has the greatest interest in this eerie tradition; Luke less so and Matthew least of all. Later, at Caesarea Philippi, Peter appears to be ignorant of it; he says only that Jesus is Messiah (8:29), not "son of the living God" (Matt 16:16).

The story of the baptism raises an interesting question. "The Spirit like a dove came down εἰς αὐτόν (1:10). This is almost always translated "to him" but the words can naturally mean "into him." The voice from heaven, "You are my Son, the beloved," follows immediately. Did Mark believe that Jesus' sonship began at this point instead of at his conception, as in Matthew and Luke? If Mark is the earliest of the gospels, this can be ascribed to a naïve adoptionism; otherwise the evangelist makes a conscious and deliberate attempt at a different Christology.[16]

At all events, nothing prior to Jesus' baptism seems to have been relevant to Mark's purpose. In the early chapters, the mighty deeds and teaching of Jesus were probably designed to portray him as Son of God and herald (perhaps bringer) of the Kingdom. In this Mark is similar to Matthew and Luke.

The Marcan Jesus, however, seldom refers to God as his Father; contrast, e.g., Matt 7:21, 10:32–33, 18:19, 20:28, 26:53, Luke 22:29, 23:46, and especially Matt 10:24–30 = Luke 10:21–22. The exceptions are Mark 8:48, 13:32 and of course the Gethsemane scene (14:32–42) with its echoes of the Lord's Prayer.[17] The GH might account for this by saying that in Mark the nature of Jesus remains hidden from the disciples.

Mark is unlike Luke in that the disciples do not address Jesus as κύριε. When the Syrophoenician woman does so, this should be understood as "Sir" (7:28). The disciples say διδάσκαλε or ῥαββεί (9:5, 11:21, 14:45, Judas); ῥαββουνί (10:51, Bartimaeus). The disciples speak of Jesus as ὁ κύριος only when they are borrowing the colt (11:3); here he is the master or boss.

---

[16] The only other evidence in the Synoptic gospels for adoptionism is in a variant in Luke 3:22, read by some OL MSS and a variety of Fathers, "You are my Son, today I have begotten you." This reading, if taken literally, and not merely as a quotation of Ps 2:7, does not fit with Luke's theology of Jesus' conception. But cf. J. D. Kingsbury, *The Christology of Mark's Gospel* (Philadelphia: Fortress, 1983) 61–65, for an argument against my position regarding Mark 1:10.

[17] The style, "your Father," so common in Matthew, is infrequent in Mark.

Jesus as Messiah in Mark

One of the most curious features of Mark's Christological language is that he is so reserved in his use of the word χριστός.[18] After 1:1 it does not appear in the gospel until 8:29, and when Peter says "You are the Messiah," Jesus "ordered them to say nothing about him" and declared instead that it was necessary for the Son Man to suffer (8:30–31). The title does appear in the *incipit*; this, however, need only indicate that Mark accepts the universal Christian designation, while "Son of Man" and "Son of God" express his understanding of it.

In the dialogue 12:35–37 Jesus quotes Ps 110:1, the familiar Christian proof text, in order to prove that the Messiah is David's Lord, not his son. Thus, if Jesus is at all descended from David, he is much more; and it is possible that Mark rejects the formula "Messiah son of David" completely.

One may ask if this is because of a Jewish tradition that Solomon, son of David, exorcised demons. Dennis Duling, in discussing this, notes that Mark puts considerable emphasis on Jesus' exorcisms, while Matthew replaces this with some general statements about Jesus' therapeutic activity.[19] Mark, therefore might reject the idea that Jesus, in being son of David, is like Solomon. But it is Matthew who multiplies "son of David" references. The only time in Mark when Jesus is addressed as son of David it is by Bartimaeus (10:47–48). When the latter cries out he is only a blind man seeking help; but after his eyes are opened he becomes a disciple. Here there is no suggestion of an exorcism, rather it is the man's faith which makes it possible for him to be healed.

The mystery in Mark is not so much a "messianic secret" as a Christological one, and what we have in 12:35–37 is a rejection of mes-

---

[18] In 1:34, Jesus "did not permit the demons to speak because they knew him." Some MSS add "to be the Messiah," but this reading should be rejected because elsewhere the demons address him as "Jesus Nazarene" (1:24) or "Jesus Son of God Most High" (5:7). For a position contrary to mine, see Kingsbury, *Christology of Mark's Gospel*, 149–50. Like many exegetes he holds that in Mark Jesus is indeed the Messiah son of David, but much more; he wields his royal authority not as a warrior king but in order to use this to have mercy on one who is afflicted. Kingsbury argues that Mark's Christology is corrective in nature (25–45). Cf. also J. D. Kingsbury, *Conflict in Mark: Jesus, Authorities, Disciples* (Minneapolis: Fortress, 1989) 45–46.

[19] D. C. Duling, "The Therapeutic Son of David; an Element in Matthew's Christological Apologetic," *NTS* 24 (1978) 392–410. This article gives full bibliography. Duling accepts the 2DH and throughout gives arguments based on Matthew's redaction of Mark and Q. If one were to accept the GH it would be necessary to answer many of these.

sianic language in connection with this mystery. Similarly, when the people welcome Jesus with the shout, "Blessed is the coming kingdom of our father David" (11:10), they do not know the full truth about Jesus' nature and mission.

There is, of course, the curious verse 9:41 ("because you belong to Christ") which is appended to the pericope of the Outsider Exorcist. Luke has no parallel to this verse, and Matthew does not have the pericope at all. There is no textual problem about the verse, but it looks like an early intrusion into the text from Matt 10:42.

The eschatological discourse uses the word in ways that do not refer to Jesus. There are warnings against those who say, "See, here is the Messiah, or there" and against false messiahs and false prophets (13:21–22). Elsewhere the term is used by Jesus' enemies. In 14:61–62 the high priest asks Jesus if he is the Messiah, the son of the Blessed; and while Jesus answers, "I am," he refers to himself as the Son of Man. The parallel Matt 26:63–64 reads "Messiah the Son of God" and Jesus gives the ambiguous answer, σὺ εἶπας, and Luke 22:67–68 rewrites the dialogue. Mark, in using the pious circumlocution "the Blessed," appears to be more original. In the crucifixion story the chief priest and scribes taunt Jesus, "Let the Messiah, the king of Israel, come down form the cross" (15:32).

Caesarea Philippi in Mark

The manner in which Mark prepares for the message that the Son of Man must suffer is in sharper contrast to the composition of Matthew and Luke. The latter use the title more often and miscellaneously prior to the scene at Caesarea Philippi. Indeed in the Sign of Jonah pericope, where Jesus is Son of Man, there is a hint of his death and resurrection. Up to 8:27 in Mark the phrase appears only twice. The Son of Man on earth has authority to forgive sins (2:10), and the Son of Man is lord (or master) of the sabbath (2:28). These two verses, which outsiders might have understood only as self-designations, set the stage for a future disclosure of the mystery at the time of Peter's confession.

The differences between the pericope itself (Mark 8:27–9:1) and its parallels (Matt 16:13–28 and Luke 9:18–27) are also significant.

First, Jesus' question to the disciples in Matt 16:13 reads, "Who do people say that the Son of Man is?" Cf. Mark 8:27, "Who do people say that I am?" and Luke 9:18, "Who do the crowds say that I am?" In Matthew's form, "Son of Man" can be only a self-designation anticipating the use of the phrase in vv. 27–28.

Second, in all three gospels the Passion predictions begin after Peter's confession, but in Matt 16:21 "Son of Man" does not appear; contrast Mark 8:31, Luke 9:22. This breaks the symmetry of the three predictions, and it is probably Matthew who has made the change.[20]

Each of the Passion predictions is followed by a discourse.[21] The first of these calls for loyal confession of Jesus and following the way of the Cross. Thus the Jesus of Mark rejects any theology which denies the suffering of the Son of Man, any discipleship in which one tries to protect one's own life, and in fact a religion of success. The only question concerns Mark's attitude to the miracles recorded in Chaps. 1–8, which the evangelist seems to tell with delight.

The theme of the Reign of God is by no means forgotten, for the discourse concludes with a promise of the coming of the Kingdom (9:1). Matt 16:28 reads, "Truly I tell you, there are some of those who stand (ἐστώτων) here who will not taste death before they see the Son of Man coming in his kingdom." Luke reads ἀληθῶς instead of ἀμήν, and concludes "before they see the Kingdom of God." Mark has ἀμήν and Luke's ἑστηκότων, and the saying ends, "before they see the Kingdom of God ἐληλυθυῖαν ἐν δυνάμει. Here Mark is the middle term. What is striking in Mark is the statement of the powerful presence of the Kingdom of God that is to come.

Matthew's idea that the Son of Man will judge and that he has a kingdom of his own is in harmony with the teachings of the parables of the Weeds and the Seine. I conclude that Matthew and Luke are here dependent on Mark.

Q as a Coherent Document

Before one takes up the Christology of Q, it is necessary to show that the case for Q is strong enough to permit such a discussion.

---

[20] Cf. Matt 10:32, where Jesus says "I," but Luke 12:8 has "the Son of Man." It is not clear why Matt 16:21 and Luke 9:21 have ἐγερθῆναι while Mark 8:31 reads ἀναστῆναι. This is one of the "minor agreements." But note use of the verb ἐγείρω in Matt 27:64, 28:7 and Luke 24:6, 34. Luke, however, uses ἀναστήσεται in 18:33 (third Passion prediction), 24:7. Acts 2:24, 32; 3:26 employ this verb, but God is the subject. Tuckett does not discuss this pericope as a whole but he does mention the peculiarity (*The Revival of the Griesbach Hypothesis: An Analysis and Appraisal* [Cambridge: Cambridge University Press, 1985] 66–67).

[21] I mentioned this pattern in 1960; see S. E. Johnson, *A Commentary on the Gospel according to St. Mark* (London: Black, 1960) 162. Norman Perrin developed this further; cf. N. Perrin and D. C. Duling, *The New Testament: An Introduction* (2nd ed.; New York: Harcourt Brace Jovanovich, 1982) 248–49.

The basic argument against the Q hypothesis is that Luke's use of Matthew is a better explanation of the phenomena. Long ago, Austin Farrer gave five principal arguments against the impossibility of Luke having used Matthew.[22]

Farrer's first point is well taken. It is futile to argue that in Matthew there are items that Luke would not have omitted had he known them. The second point that Farrer denies is that Luke appears more "primitive." That is certainly true with respect to the two gospels as a whole. It is difficult to find a good criterion for judging what is primitive, but some of Luke's special material seems to be very early, and I shall argue that the reconstructed Q has a *distinctive* theology which is at least as primitive as that of Mark.

Third, Farrer holds that Luke used Mark (against the GH), adopted Mark's general order, and quarried Matthew for small pieces which he put into a mosaic of his own. The answer to this is that the reconstructed Q is coherent and not derived solely from Luke.

Fourth, Farrer rejects the argument that the order in which Luke places the common Matthew-Luke material is mostly less appropriate than the order that it has in Matthew. His answer is that Luke wrote his gospel to please himself, not us moderns. Of course this is so, but (1) the result is that both gospels as they stand are rather miscellaneous, and (2) that in the reconstructed Q the material is more coherent than in either of the two gospels.

Fifth, Farrer answers the point that the common (Q) material is placed in Marcan pericopes in Matthew, while Luke puts it elsewhere. He holds instead that Luke follows Mark without the Matthaean additions, and collects the latter elsewhere. That is, Luke's gospel is a critical reworking and rewriting of Mark. Farrer explains the structure of Luke as similar to that of Matthew but distinct. He adopts Evans' understanding of the Central Section of Luke as Luke's Deuteronomy, but goes further. The gospel is a Hexateuch based on a typology of Genesis to Joshua. This is very ingenious, for the gospel contains many types, particularly in the first two chapters, but it is almost too subtle, and we have seen that there are other ways of understanding Luke's structure and methods.

In his major article on Q, Arland D. Jacobson answers Farmer's form of the argument. He notes first that there is general agreement that the

---

22   A. M. Farrer, "On Dispensing with Q," *Studies in the Gospels* (ed. D. E. Nineham; Oxford: Blackwell, 1955) 55–88, especially 63–81. Cf. also E. C. Hobbs, "A Quarter-Century without Q," *Perkins Journal* 33.4 (Summer 1986) 10–19.

three gospels "stand in some kind of literary relationship to one another" (Step I), but argues that what Farmer does in Step II is to propose one hypothesis, the GH, to explain another hypothesis, i.e., direct copying of one gospel by another, and that is to beg the question. As to Step III, the rejection of an appeal to hypothetical documents, it was precisely the weakness of the theory that Luke used Matthew which led to the Q hypothesis in the first place. Further, Farmer himself posits a number of hypothetical sources. Lastly, the "minor agreements" between Matthew and Luke do not arise from a single cause.[23]

These answers to the GH would not be sufficient in themselves to demonstrate the superiority of the 2DH and specifically the Q hypothesis. The strength of Jacobson's article is his use of form criticism to disclose the distinctive literary forms of Q. Macarisms are common in Q but rare in Mark; there are at least nine woes in Q, but none in Mark; four eschatological correlations in Q, none in Mark; while Q "has a disproportionate number of prophetic threats." On the other hand, several forms are common in Mark but rare in Q. In Mark there are eleven conflict stories, but the only one in Q is the Beelzebul controversy. The only miracle stories in Q are Luke 7:1–10 = Matt 8:5–13 and Luke 11:14 = Matt 12:22–23a. The former is not a typical miracle story, and the latter serves as a setting for the Beelzebul controversy. Both Mark and Q include parables, but those in Q have an eschatological setting.[24]

Jacobson finds the unity of Q in the fact that it stands within a prophetic tradition, specifically the deuteronomistic tradition of the history of Israel's disobedience. Wisdom sends the prophets who are rejected. [25]

The case for Q rests finally on the observation that, when Q is reconstructed, it turns out to be a coherent document with a theology of its own, independent of the three Synoptic gospels. Kloppenborg's book is now the most complete and persuasive demonstration of this subject, the literature of which is very large. He has reviewed previous discussions, from the 19th century on, including Robinson's seminal article,[26] and has

---

[23] A. D. Jacobson, "The Literary Unity of Q," *JBL* 101 (1982) 365–89, especially 369–71. On the "minor agreements" he follows Neirynck (F. Neirynck with Theo Hansen and F. Van Segbroeck [eds.], *The Minor Agreements of Matthew and Luke against Mark with a Cumulative List* [BETL 39; Gembloux/Louvain: Duculot/Leuven University Press, 1974]). Jacobson also reviews much of recent literature on Q.

[24] Jacobson, "Literary Unity," 373–78.

[25] Jacobson, "Literary Unity," 383–88.

[26] LOGOI SOPHON: On the Gattung of Q," in J. M. Robinson and H. Koester, *Trajectories through Early Christianity* (Philadelphia: Fortress, 1971) 71–113. See now,

built on the insights of Jacobson and many other scholars, and finally has located Q in the tradition of ancient sayings collections.[27]

It becomes evident at once that, while scholars differ in details of their reconstructions of Q, there is a fair amount of agreement as to its content, its order, and the themes with which it deals.[28]

Christology in the Q Material

The earlier part of this chapter concentrated on the Christology of the three gospels in their final form. I have, however, remarked on some sayings in which Jesus is Son of God or Son of Man which are usually assigned to Q. Without attempting a complete analysis of Christology in the Q material, it is desirable to note some of its characteristics.

Jesus' sonship to God is stated in the strongest terms in Luke 10:21–22 (=Matt 11:25–28), first in his thanksgiving to the Father and then in the claim to a unique and comprehensive revelation. The temptation story is unique in the Q material in its form and may belong to the latest stage in the development of Q. Again Jesus is Son of God, though it is the tempter who challenges him with this title. His renunciation of the easy ways to establish his authority serves "to illustrate and legitimate the mode of behavior and the authority of the Q group." As a story of testing or

---

Adela Yarbro Collins, "The Son of Man Sayings in the Sayings Source," in *To Touch the Text: Biblical and Related Studies in Honor of Joseph A. Fitzmyer, S. J.* (ed. Maurya P. Horgan and Paul J. Kobelski; New York: Crossroad, 1989) 369–89. Here she reviews Robinson's article and also that of Koester in the same volume, together with discussions by Tödt, Lührmann and Schürmann, and concludes that the *logoi sophōn* are not merely proverbial or didactic wisdom, but belong also to the apocalyptic tradition. The sayings on the future coming of the Son of Man are among the most primitive of the post-Easter formulations. Discussions in this article provide one more indication that Q was an actual document.

[27] John S. Kloppenborg, *The Formation of Q: Trajectories in Ancient Wisdom Collections* (Philadelphia: Fortress, 1987) 263–316.

[28] Kloppenborg, *Formation of Q*, 72–79, 89–95. For other recent reconstructions see, e.g., R. A. Edwards, *The Theology of Q* (Philadelphia: Fortress, 1976); Wolfgang Schenk, *Synopse zur Redenquelle der Evangelien: Q Synopse und Rekonstruktion in deutscher Übersetzung mit kurzen Erläuterungen* (Düsseldorf: Patmos, 1981); A. Polag, *Fragmenta Q: Textheft zur Logienquelle* (Neukirchen-Vluyn: Neukirchener Verlag, 1979). Ivan Havener, *Q, The Sayings of Jesus* (Wilmington, DE: Michael Glazier, 1987) is based on Polag. On the theology of Q, see also Polag, *Die Christologie der Logienquelle* (NTAbh 8; Münster: Aschendorff, 1972). Dieter Lührmann, "The Gospel of Mark and the Sayings Collection Q," *JBL* 109 (1989) 58–59, lists points of general agreement among these scholars.

ordeal "it validates Jesus' loyalty to this original commitment."[29] These passages are generally agreed to belong to the Wisdom theme which is prominent in the Q material, from whatever source it may come. Jesus not only has access to God's will, but obeys it like a true Son.

There are also some Son of Man sayings. Their variety illustrates the statement that in Q such logia function in the interpretation of other sayings.[30] All of these are related to the Q theme of the announcement of judgment. In two of them Jesus is the rejected prophet who has nowhere to lay his head (Luke 9:58=Matt 8:20) and is scorned as a glutton and wine drinker, but Wisdom is justified by her children (Luke 7:31–35 = Matt 11:16–19). A word spoken against him can be forgiven (here he is thought of as prophet), but not one spoken against the Holy Spirit, the source of his message (Luke 12:10 = Matt 12:32). Like Jonah he is a sign to this generation. When judgment is made, the Ninevites and the Queen of the South will testify against those who reject his words, in which there is a wisdom greater than that of Solomon (Luke 11:29–32; cf. Matt 12:41–42). Another saying goes further: whoever acknowledges Jesus will be acknowledged by the Son of Man in the presence of the angels of God (Luke 12:8–9; cf. Matt 10:32–33). Finally, a Kingdom saying, in the context of the Beelzebul controversy, affirms that because Jesus casts out demons by the finger/Spirit of God, the Reign of God has arrived (Luke 11:20 = Matt 12:28).

Jesus as Prophet

In the passages just mentioned, Jesus is primarily the prophet whose message must be obeyed if one is to survive the judgment. Indeed the role of Jesus as prophet is common to all four gospels. In Matthew's account of the triumphal entry the crowds shout, "This is the prophet Jesus from Nazareth in Galilee" (21:11). When Jesus raises the widow's son at Nain, he is acclaimed as a prophet (Luke 7:15). In the Fourth Gospel his role as prophet is prominent. The Samaritan woman says, "Sir, I perceive that you are a prophet" (John 4:19), and the response of the people after he feeds the Five Thousand is, "This is truly the prophet who is to come into the world" (6:14). On another occasion, there are those who reject Jesus because a prophet cannot be expected from Galilee (7:52).[31]

[29] Kloppenborg, *Formation of Q*, 247–48, 256–62.

[30] Kloppenborg, *Formation of Q*, 99, n. 21, citing H. Schürmann (*Jesus und der Menschensohn* [Freiburg: Herder, 1975] 124–47).

[31] The question of the true prophet and the false is one of the basic themes of the Fourth Gospel; see Wayne A. Meeks, *The Prophet King* (Leiden: Brill, 1967).

In Mark, however, the theme of Jesus as prophet appears to be only a submerged motif. It is true that twice people suggest that he may be a prophet (Mark 6:15, 8:28), but this is not a sufficient interpretation of his nature and work. The most significant use of the word is in the saying in 6:4, "A prophet is not without honor except in his own fatherland." Jesus appears as a "man of God" like Elijah or Elisha in the miraculous feedings and in the raising of Jairus' daughter (cf. Luke 7:11–17). His cleansing of the Temple can be regarded as a prophetic act, and his answer to the scribes in Mark 11:27–33 implies that his authority is parallel to that of John the Baptizer. The predictions of the end in Chap. 13 are an apocalyptic form of prophecy.

Here there is a decided contrast between Mark and the Q material, for in the latter Jesus continually speaks and acts as prophet.

Both Mark and Q interpret Jesus' suffering and death, but in Q his death is in accordance with what has happened to *all* the prophets; see Luke 6:28 = Matt 5:12; Luke 11:47–48 = Matt 23:29–30, 34–35; Luke 13:34 = Matt 23:37.[32]

The pericope Luke 9:57–60 = Matt 8:19–22, in which two men offer to follow Jesus, is of particular importance, for he is pictured as a wandering prophet. Luke adds the example of a third (9:61–62) who wishes, like Elisha (1 Kings 19:20), to say good-bye to his family before accompanying Jesus. This may also have belonged to Q.[33] In Luke this prepares directly for the sending out of the Seventy-two.

Gerd Theissen has proposed the theory that the Jesus movement was originally one of "wandering radicalism," i.e., the early disciples gave up home, family, and society in general to follow a new way of life.[34]

Dieter Lührmann has, however, argued that the wandering prophets reflect rather a smaller group, the community behind Q, which took Jesus as its model. It is true that the theme appears in Mark 10:28–31 = Matt 19:29–30, but sociologically the communities of Mark and Matthew are settled and look for guidance more often to authoritative teachers than to prophets. These two short passages, and Matt 8:19–22, are exceptions to the general picture. Luke has certainly not derived 9:57–60 from Matthew; his source is Q. He does appear to be more interested than Matthew in the wandering prophets, as one can see from the

---

[32] Lührmann, "Mark and Q," 51–71, especially 64–66.

[33] Kloppenborg, *Formation of Q*, 190, n. 80.

[34] Gerd Theissen, *Sociology of Early Palestinian Christianity* (Philadelphia: Fortress, 1978) 7–30.

Central Section and from various stories in Acts, but wandering radicalism cannot be his own invention.[35]

Jesus as Judge

In the Synoptic gospels, Jesus makes decisions on legal and religious matters. One exception is when he disdains to be a judge or divider (Luke 12:14; cf. Exod 2:14). It is only in Matthew and Luke-Acts, however, that he is the eschatological judge of the living and the dead.

The clearest cases in Matthew are in 16:27, where the Son of Man at his coming will render to everyone according to his deeds, and two parables, the Weeds (13:41–43) and the Last Judgment (25:31–46). One may perhaps add the Ten Young Girls (25:1–13).

This is less obvious in Luke. The eschatological discourse concludes with the command to be ready at all times to stand in the presence of the Son of Man (21:36; cf. 18:8, "When the Son of Man comes will he find faith on the earth?"). It is in Acts that the doctrine appears most clearly. Peter says that he and the other apostles have been commanded to testify that Jesus is the one designated by God as judge of the living and the dead (Acts 10:42; cf. Paul at the Areopagus, 17:31).

Jesus is not definitely identified as judge in Q, although if "fire" refers to punishment, the Coming One will baptize with the Holy Spirit and with fire (Matt 3:12 = Luke 3:17); in Mark 1:8 it is only with the Holy Spirit. In one eschatological passage he has the function of judge or at least as witness (Luke 13:25–27; cf. Matt 7:21–27). Jacobson remarks that words relating to judgment (κρίνω, κρίσις, κριτής) are "common in Q but completely absent from Mark. Even more striking are the frequent references to the day (ἡμέρα) of judgment. Mark knows of the 'days' of tribulation and the 'day' of the Parousia but he speaks of the 'day' of judgment only once (13:32)."[36] But in that verse "that day" is not a judgment day; the context suggests that it is the day of the Son of Man.

Thus in Mark, Jesus is not the eschatological judge. Such a function is to be distinguished from his authority during his earthly ministry. When he is pictured as ruling on matters of law he is more like a rabbi, although not one recognized by the Pharisees. His forgiveness of sins (Mark 2:10) implies that God forgives.

---

[35] Lührmann, "Mark and Q," 69–71. Such groups can maintain themselves only in interaction with settled communities, as one can see from the *Didache*.

[36] Jacobson, "Literary Unity," 375–76.

Conclusion

The most significant differences between Mark and the other gospels concern the Caesarea Philippi pericope and the chapters that lead up to it. In Mark there is a "messianic secret" which perhaps should be called the "Christological secret;" i.e., the first half of the gospel prepares for the revelation that Jesus, Son of God, must be understood as the suffering Son of Man, and this is anticipated in 2:10, 28. In contrast, both in Matthew and Luke there is a completely integrated Christology which may be gradually disclosed to the disciples but is known to the readers from the outset.

Matt 1:1–16:28 and Luke 1:1–9:27 not only contain two types of Son of Man sayings (self-designation and eschatological logion) but also announcements of Jesus as Messiah son of David, and Matt 12:40 (in the sign of Jonah pericope) even alludes to Jesus' death and resurrection. Further, in Matthew, after the walking on the water the disciples hail Jesus as Son of God (14:33), whereas in Mark 6:52 their minds are still numbed.

Mark apparently rejects the title of Messiah for Jesus unless it is understood that he is also the suffering Son of Man, and he certainly does not have this honor as descendant of David. What is most striking is that the story of his baptism can be read as teaching that Jesus was adopted as God's Son at this time.

Study of Christology in the Q material likewise tends to support the 2DH. It is at least curious that Mark, unlike Matthew and Luke-Acts, does not suggest that the Son of Man is the eschatological judge. This, and the almost complete absence of the woe-form and other forms common to the Q material, establish the presumption that Matthew and Luke use Q. If, however, the GH is correct, Mark must be seen as a radical reviser of Christology.

CHAPTER EIGHT

Judaism and Hellenism in the Synoptic Gospels

The three gospels should be compared with respect to their relation to Judaism and their handling of traditions about Jesus' rulings on matters of Torah.

Parties in Judaism

The Synoptic gospels mention Pharisees and Sadducees as groups within the Jewish community. There are also scribes (γραμματεῖς). The Sadducees are called a αἵρεσις in Acts 5:17; so are the Pharisees (15:5) and the Christians (24:5, "Nazoraeans;" 24:14; 26:5; 28:22). Josephus uses this word in referring to Pharisees, Sadducees, Essenes, and a fourth group which is like the Pharisees except that it is revolutionary.[1] "Sect" is not a good translation. In other literature αἵρεσις often denotes a philosophical school. Perhaps "party" will do for our purposes. In Josephus, Pharisees and Sadducees are distinguished by doctrines and ways of life, but most often they are political interest groups.[2]

---

[1] For Josephus' descriptions, see *Ant.* 13.5.7 §173; 18.1.2 §11; *Vita* 10.

[2] Anthony J. Saldarini, *Pharisees, Scribes and Sadducees in Palestinian Society: A Sociological Approach* (Wilmington, DE: Michael Glazier, 1988) 120–27. Saldarini never speaks of "parties" and prefers "groups." This is the most recent full treatment of groupings in Palestine. Dieter Lührmann has also made a distinction between Pharisees and scribes ("Die Pharisäer und die Schriftgelehrte im Markusevangelium," *ZNW* 78 [1987] 169–85). J. D. Kingsbury, "The Religious Authorities in the Gospel of Mark," *NTS* 36 (1990) 42–65, rejects this distinction as artificial. Mark's purpose, he says, is to show that all the religious authorities plus the Herodians form a common front against Jesus. The "friendly scribe" is an ironic character, and Joseph of Arimathaea is not one of the "religious authorities." E. S. Malbon, "The Jewish Leaders in the Gospel of Mark: A Literary Study of Marcan Characterization," *JBL* 108 (1989) 259–81, holds that as in much ancient literature such

The scribes were a definite group, but the NT never refers to them as a αἵρεσις. They probably do not have common doctrines or purposes; evidently they are people of some learning and influence but they cut across other classifications. Mark speaks once of the "scribes of the Pharisees" (2:16); obviously not all scribes are Pharisees, nor are all Pharisees scribes.

The NT never mentions the Essenes. There are, however, Herodians (Mark 3:6, 12:13 = Matt 22:16). These are certainly a political group who in Jesus' times were probably partisans of Herod Antipas. A. J. Saldarini regards all the opponents of Jesus in the gospels, Pharisees, Sadducees, scribes, Herodians, and some of the priests, as members of the "retainer class," subordinate to the ruling class, but superior in status and influence to merchants, artisans, and peasants.[3]

The evangelists evidently know less about the Sadducees, except that they deny the resurrection (Matt 22:23, Mark 12:18, Luke 20:27, Acts 23:6–8). If they know that the high priest and his friends are Sadducees, Mark and Matthew do not bother to say so. Luke knows that there are Sadducees in the Sanhedrin (Acts 4:1, 5:17). Otherwise it is Matthew who most frequently mentions this group. He couples them with Pharisees (3:7; 16:1, 6, 12); of course in 22:34 they are implicitly contrasted with the Pharisees.

One should note particularly that in Mark 8:15, in the discourse on the loaves, Jesus warns against the leaven of the Pharisees and the leaven of Herod, while Matt 16:6 substitutes the Sadducees for Herod.[4]

In general the Synoptic gospels use "scribes and Pharisees" as a stock phrase and blur the distinction between them. In particular Matt 24 contains a series of woes against "scribes and Pharisees, hypocrites;" cf. Matt

---

groups are treated as types, although Mark does not absolutize the schema. She agrees that the groups of opponents are lumped together. This does not, however, remove the probability that Mark has some knowledge of the Herodians and, unlike Matthew and Luke, is interested in their political stance.

3 Saldarini, *Pharisees, Scribes and Sadducees*, 42–43, 267–80. See also A. J. Hultgren, *Jesus and His Adversaries* (Minneapolis: Augsburg, 1979) 154–56.

4 Quentin Quesnell, *The Mind of Mark* (Rome: Pontifical Biblical Institute, 1969) 243–57, explains the reference to Herod from the passages referring to Herod and John the Baptizer, i.e., Herod represents the people who listened to Jesus gladly (12:27; cf. 6:20b) but were easily swayed and did not recognize who he was. W. H. Kelber's solution (*The Kingdom in Mark* [Philadelphia: Fortress, 1974] 61–62) is that what the Pharisees and Herod had in common was their opposition to the Kingdom of God. These theological explanations of Mark's purpose do not rule out a tradition about the political situation.

5:20. Luke speaks often of scribes and Pharisees or Pharisees and scribes, and sometimes associates scribes with chief priests and elders. He also mentions νομικοί, perhaps "experts in the law" (7:30). Mark never uses the word, Matthew only in 22:35 (=Luke 10:25, a "minor agreement"). This is a more precise word designating scribes (literate people) who have a particular specialty. Jesus denounces the Pharisees in Luke 11:37–44 for their rulings on cleanliness and tithes, their desire for prestige, and their hypocrisy, and then turns to the other group, who lay heavy burdens on others and have taken away the key of knowledge (11:45–52). In 14:3 they are coupled with the Pharisees when Jesus asks if it is lawful to heal on the sabbath.

There is, however, a good lawyer who gives the summary of the law (Luke 10:25–28); likewise in Mark 12:28–34 a scribe approves enthusiastically of Jesus' similar summary and is told that he is not far from the Reign of God. When some Pharisees warn Jesus about Herod's hostility, we are not sure whether Luke thinks of them as friendly (13:31), but in Acts there are Christian Pharisees (15:5), and Paul claims to be one of them (23:7).

Saldarini finds that of the three Synoptists it is Mark who most clearly distinguished between Pharisees and scribes. The two groups have certain interests in common, but the Pharisees are especially concerned about such issues as fasting, the purity and food laws, and sabbath observance. When the scribes are mentioned the emphasis is on their authority; they seem to be recognized teachers, perhaps somewhat like the later rabbis.[5]

These distinctions are obscured in Matthew. The "scribes of the Pharisees" (Mark 2:16) are just Pharisees in Matt 9:11, and the scribes from Jerusalem (Mark 3:22) become Pharisees (Matt 9:34, 12:24). Chief priests, scribes, and elders are mentioned in Mark 11:27; Matt 21:28 has chief priests and elders; Luke 20:1, priests, scribes, and elders. In Mark 12:28–34 the scribe is friendly, as we have noted, but in Matt 22:34–35 the question is asked by a lawyer who is among the group of Pharisees who have come together after Jesus has silenced the Sadducees. There is one exception. The Pharisees put Jesus to the test by asking for a sign (Mark 8:11), but in one parallel Matthew adds Sadducees (16:1) and in another it is certain of the scribes and Pharisees (12:38).[6]

---

5 Saldarini, *Pharisees, Scribes and Sadducees*, 155.
6 Saldarini, *Pharisees, Scribes and Sadducees*, 163–64.

Luke often adds a mention of the Pharisees. As we have noted, he sometimes exhibits some sympathy toward them, but in his special materials they are given an unfavorable character (7:36–50, 18:9–14). The "ruler" who belongs to the Pharisees (14:1) appears to be a person of authority. The group has contacts with Herod Antipas (13:31), and Luke even accuses the Pharisees of loving money (16:14).[7]

If, as the GH assumes, Mark uses Matthew and Luke, it is necessary to explain why he changes "Pharisees" to "scribes" and indicates that the latter are especially powerful opponents. It is even more curious that Jesus, instead of warning against the leaven of the Pharisees and Sadducees, presumably their false teaching or behavior (Matt 16:6), he should speak of the leaven of Herod (Mark 8:15). This, and Mark's two mentions of the Herodians as hostile (3:6, 12:13), suggests that Mark has, at least in this respect, a greater knowledge than Matthew and Luke of the political situation in Jesus' time.[8] Finally, Mark does not adopt Luke's picture of the Pharisees as wealthy or money loving.

Legal Sayings

Parts of the Sermon on the Mount are concerned with Torah and its interpretation.

The statement on the permanence of the law (5:17–20) is much more developed than in the parallel in Luke 16:16–17 and is used to introduce a series of antitheses.

Torah as a whole contains both halakhah and aggadah, and the antitheses include both types. Some sayings are purely ethical and could not have been enforced by a court: murder and anger (5:21–22), adultery and lust (5:27–28); non-resistance (5:38–42 = Luke 6:29–30), and love of enemies (5:43–48 = Luke 6:21–28, 32–36).

The two legal sayings concern divorce (5:31–32) and oaths (5:33–37). The first of these has a doublet in 19:9 (=Mark 10:11) and a parallel in Luke 16:18. Luke has nothing corresponding to the dialogue in 19:3–8. His saying is in a cluster which comes immediately after that passage, evidently editorial, in which the Pharisees are criticized for their love of money and their pride. The result of this combination is that the law is

---

[7] Saldarini, *Pharisees, Scribes and Sadducees*, 174–76.

[8] Saldarini holds to the priority of Mark and believes that Mark's traditions probably date to the middle of the 1st century (*Pharisees, Scribes and Sadducees*, 145). Most of the Pharisees were subordinate officials, bureaucrats, judges, and educators who had a program for society (284), but neither Pharisees nor scribes had a stable social status; they belonged to the retainer class (282).

deemed good but the Pharisees bad. First there is a saying contrasting the era of the law and the prophets with the age of Jesus and John when the reign of God is proclaimed (16:16 = Matt 11:12–13). Although this is a new age, there follows the categorical statement on the permanence of the law (16:17 = Matt 5:18–19). Finally divorce is forbidden absolutely (16:18).

Both Matt 5:32 and Luke 16:18 are written from the Jewish point of view, i.e., that the man does the marrying. Both say that whoever marries the woman who is divorced commits adultery. Matthew, however, does not condemn a man who divorces his wife in the case of a λόγος πορνείας (perhaps the "shameful thing" as understood by the school of Shammai); the point is that if he divorces his wife for any other reason he causes her to commit adultery (perhaps by another marriage) because she is still married to him. In Luke, any man who divorces his wife for any reason at all and marries another is an adulterer.

Here supporters of the GH might argue either that (1) Luke draws upon Matt 5:32 but rejects the exception clause and ignores the sin of the divorced wife so as to forbid any man to marry a divorced wife; or (2) that Luke has an independent logion. If Luke has been using Matthew, he curiously puts it into the context of the Reign of God and the permanence of the law.

The situation is quite different in Matt 19:9 and Mark 10:11, for the two gospels are in clearer literary relationship at this point. They differ slightly at the beginning (Matthew, λέγω δὲ ὑμῖν; Mark, καὶ λέγει αὐτοῖς) but the kernel saying is the same except that Mark does not have the exception clause μὴ ἐπὶ πορνείᾳ and at the end adds ἐπ᾿αὐτήν and v. 12. Matthew has in mind what he said in 5:32 and makes the point that was omitted there, namely, that a man must not divorce his wife and marry another except in this one case.

Matthew is dealing with what his church considers a difficult situation and this is shown especially by the fact that he adds a dialogue on eunuchs or celibates. Since one cannot usually get a divorce, should one marry at all?

One might argue from the GH that Mark, influenced by Luke 16:18, simply deletes μη ἐπὶ πορνείᾳ and says further that for a man to marry another woman is an offense against his true wife. The literary relationships look different from the perspective of the 2DH. Matt 19:3–12 is a unified pericope, the additions being marked only by λέγω δὲ ὑμῖν in verse 9 and the answer of the disciples in verse 10.[9] But Mark 10:2–9 is self-contained and vv.10–11 are a private teaching given when the disciples in the house ask Jesus about his answer to the Pharisees. The question of the latter had been whether a man might divorce his wife, whereas in Matt 19:3 it was "for any cause" (the issue between Shammai and Hillel). The teaching in Mark 10:2–9 is strict as in Luke 16:18, and verses 10–12 appear to be a separate and appended tradition. Matthew's pericope can therefore be derived from Mark and modified according to Matt 5:32.

In addition, Mark thinks of a situation in which the wife divorces her husband (10:12). Paul also presumes that this is possible (1 Cor 7:10–11). Most commentators suggest that this reflects Roman society and civil law rather than a Jewish milieu, but Bernadette Brooten has argued persuasively that Paul and Mark represent a Torah ruling belonging to Judaism in Palestine. Two passages in the Elephantine papyri (5th century B.C.) assume that a wife can divorce her husband. Josephus tells of three women of the Herodian family who did so. Two passages in the Talmud specify that this is possible if it has been provided for in the marriage contract. Brooten concludes that in 1st century Palestine there were two legal opinions on the matter, and that Mark and Paul reflect the earlier of the two traditions.[10]

Mark 10:12 thus does not indicate that Mark is more or less Hellenistic than the other gospels. It does, however, suggest that here Mark is independent of Matthew and Luke, and in fact that Mark has not

---

[9] The OT quotations do not give clear evidence in favor of the GH or the 2DH. Jesus responds to the Pharisees' question (Mark 10:3) by asking what Moses commanded, and they respond with a brief summary of Deut 24:1, probably derived from the LXX, a verse that contains the verbs γράφω and δίδωμι. Mark chooses the first (10:4) and Matthew the second (19:7). This kind of dialogue is found in all three gospels, e.g., Mark 3:23 = Matt 12:3, "have you never read?" (cf. Mark 9:12, "and how is it written?" 11:17, "is it not written?"). In Luke 10:26 Jesus asks what is written, and in Matt 21:42 = Mark 12:10 = Luke 20:17 all three gospels precede a quotation with Jesus' question.

In Mark the quotation from Deuteronomy precedes the one from Gen 2:24 instead of following it. Here the citation from the LXX is identical in the two gospels except that Matt 19:5 adds καὶ κολληθήσεται τῇ γυναικὶ αὐτοῦ. Here the opponents quote Moses' provision in answer to Jesus' argument from Genesis. It is not certain which form of the dialogue is the more effective.

[10] Bernadette Brooten, "Konnten Frauen im alten Judentum die Scheidung betreiben?" *EvT* 42 (1982) 65–80. She correctly remarks that scholarship has not paid sufficient attention to the status of women and their daily life in ancient Judaism. See also note 32 to Chap. 1.

revised Matthew; it is rather that Matthew reflects the tradition of the Jewish community known to him.

The prohibition of oaths is legal in character and its theme is further developed in Matt 23:16–22. There is evidence that occasionally a rabbi used a legal argument to render a provision of Torah inoperative.[11] These pericopes are sufficient to show how much Matthew is in touch with discussions of a rabbinical type.

One dialogue, Matt 17:24–27, on the Temple tax, is at first sight startling because it seems almost like a Pauline principle: God's sons are free, but in order to avoid scandal, they should pay the tax. When Matthew wrote, the Temple had ceased to exist and the tax was collected by the Roman government. The pericope may reflect a situation in which Jewish Christians wondered whether they should pay; at the same time it affirms Jesus' loyalty to the Temple and the good citizenship of Christians.

In this dialogue Peter, as representing the community, is the interlocutor. This fits with the saying 16:18–19, in which Jesus bestows on Peter the keys of the Kingdom and the power to bind and loose. The latter probably refers to declaring something forbidden or permitted.[12]

In 18:18 the prerogative of binding and loosing is committed to the local church and extended to include power to excommunicate. 18:15–20 develops the biblical rule of two or three witnesses to apply to personal wrongs done in the community. Here we have the beginnings of a Christian legal system.[13]

Woes on Scribes and Pharisees

The denunciation of the scribes and Pharisees (23:1–36) is composite, contains paraenesis along with legal materials, and some parts of it are peculiar to Matthew. First, the scribes and Pharisees sit in Moses' seat, their commands are to be obeyed, but the disciples must not imitate their hypocritical behavior (23:2–3). This is surprising, because Jesus is the only true authority; it may be that Matthew's church is in close contact

---

[11] H. L. Strack and P. Billerbeck, *Kommentar zum Neuen Testament aus Talmud und Midrasch* (Munich: C. H. Beck, 1922) 717 on Matt 15:6.

[12] See, e.g., K. Stendahl, *PCB*, 687b.

[13] Matthew puts into this context a logion on prayer (18:19–20) very much like the rabbinic saying in *Aboth* 3:2 that where two or three are gathered and there are words of Torah among them, the Shekinah is present. The process of judgment is overseen by Jesus, who is present as Lord of his Church, and judgment must be balanced by unlimited forgiveness (18:21–35).

with a powerful Jewish community and, as in the case of the Temple tax, is warned not to give unnecessary offense.

The scribes and Pharisees make their phylacteries broad and enlarge their tassels (κράσπεδα, 23:5). Farmer, following Rengstorf, supposes that Mark in 12:38 has changed Matthew's φυλακτήρια to στολαί, which might mean "long garments." Tuckett makes an apt criticism of this notion.[14] The disciples are not to be called Rabbi, father or teacher (23:8–10) and Matthew brings in the saying on servanthood which was developed in 20:26–28 and its parallels. The opponents are also criticized for their zeal in enlisting proselytes (23:15) and for their casuistry on oaths (23:16–22). They strain out a gnat but swallow a camel (23:24). If Luke knew Matthew, it is curious that he did not include this last saying.

Thus in his special material Matthew stands for the permanence of the law and even counsels some obedience to Pharisaic teachers, though he abhors their zeal, their fine distinctions and their concern for what Jesus regards as trifles. He also believes that the Church, as represented by Peter, has the power to make legal decisions. There are to be no individual rabbis; interpretation of the law rests on Jesus' words and is a community matter. Yet Matthew transmits a parable ascribed to Jesus: a scribe who has been made disciple to the Kingdom of the heavens brings out treasures that are *new* as well as old (13:52). This is a good description of Matthew himself.

Mark and Luke on Torah

On the basis of the GH, it could certainly be argued that Mark deliberately ignores the inconsistencies in Jesus' attitude to Torah as portrayed in Matthew. But since he rejected the Pharisees' oral law and criticized them for hypocrisy, he could have found more powerful material in Matthew than he included in the somewhat confusing arguments of Mark 7:1–19. As to the denunciations in 12:38–40, he might have considered that he had said enough, but, as we have seen, it is difficult to suppose that he has drawn this from Matthew.

I have previously noted that the whole of Mark 2 is unified by the contrast between the old and the new, and that the fasts mentioned in 2:18–20 are probably the voluntary Monday and Thursday observances

---

[14] C. M. Tuckett, *The Revival of the Griesbach Hypothesis: An Analysis and Appraisal* (Cambridge: Cambridge University Press, 1983) 136–37.

that were a mark of piety but not strictly required.[15] The other evangelists include this pericope with the radical sayings on the patch on the
old cloak and the new wine in old skins (Matt 9:14–17 = Luke 5:33–39).
Mark introduces this as a question raised by the disciples of John and of
the Pharisees, Matthew more briefly, with his characteristic τότε
προσέρχονται αὐτῷ. Luke makes the issue a question raised by Jesus' own
disciples and adds the curious v. 39 at the end ("the old wine is good").
Mark seems to provide the best setting for the scene, and the forms in the
other gospels are best explained as the editing of Mark's pericope.

What is most striking here is that none of the three evangelists is conscious of a distinction between what Torah demands and what rabbinic
tradition recommends. When the Sermon on the Mount discusses the
proper way to fast (Matt 6:16–18), the reference may be to any public
fasts. In 11:13, Matthew reads, "For all the prophets and the law prophe-
sied until John" and in 5:17 the law and the prophets are not annulled by
Jesus. Thus, if Matthew classified all rules for fasting as Torah, he does
not seem to perceive an inconsistency when Jesus finds fasting inappro-
priate (cf. also the contrast between John and Jesus in Matt 11:18–19).

It is conceivable that Mark is secondary here, but if so he has borrowed words almost equally from Matthew and Luke. The most reasonable solution is that both are editing Mark.

There are other passages containing material common to Matthew
and Mark. Matthew's form of the plucking of grain on the Sabbath (12:1–
8 = Mark 2:23–28 = Luke 6:1–5) contains some peculiarities. In addition to
citing the example of David, it is argued that the priests work in the
Temple.[16] Jesus quotes Hos 6:6, "I desire mercy and not sacrifice." It is
not clear why Luke would omit this if he was using Matthew, unless he
decided that the David example was sufficient to produce a tight, convincing apophthegm. Even more surprising is Mark's mistaken reference
to Abiathar (2:26) and his inclusion of 2:27, "The Sabbath came into being
for human beings, not human beings for the Sabbath." This proverb,
which has a 2nd century rabbinic parallel (R. Simeon b. Menasya, *Mekilta*
on Exod 31:14), fits the point of the incident in David's story and may be
pre-Marcan. 2:28, "The Son of Man is lord of the Sabbath," reflects
Mark's theology, and it can be argued that Matthew and Luke indepen-
dently prefer to include this saying rather than the other.

---

[15] D. Daube, "Responsibilities of Master and Disciples in the Gospels," *NTS* 19
(1972) 1–15, especially 4.
[16] Tuckett, *Griesbach Hypothesis*, 129–30 and n. 30 cites this as showing that
Matthew regards the OT law as in force.

The situation is similar in the next pericope, the healing of the man with the withered hand (Matt 12:9–14 = Mark 3:1–6 = Luke 6:6–11). If Mark is copying either, he has chosen Luke; the opponents are watching Jesus to see what he will do, and Jesus asks the infuriating question, "Is it lawful to do good on the Sabbath or to do evil?" Matthew, however, justifies Jesus' loyalty to the law by introducing the case of a man who has a sheep fallen into a pit, using the argument from the light to the heavy (12:11–12a).

Luke 14:5, which occurs in the story of the dropsical man (14:1–6), has some similarity to the Matthew pericope just mentioned. Here it is the case of an ox fallen into a well. A more distant parallel occurs in Luke 13:10–17, the story of the crippled woman. This mentions loosing an ox or an ass to feed on the Sabbath. Tuckett discusses the GH and the more satisfactory solution of the 2DH.[17]

This is another case in which Matthew justifies Jesus' action by a legal argument. Luke has less interest in such arguments, and the two Lucan miracles are an exception to this general method. These stories are of interest to him because they exhibit Jesus as the liberator, a theme which comes out clearly in 13:10–17. It is possible that Matt 12:11–12a and Luke 14:5 derive from a common source. Mark's story is consistent, although the argument in Mark 3:4 could not have been accepted by Jesus' opponents. Matthew tries to deal with this problem but fails to be logically convincing.

Tuckett also discusses the controversy over the clean and the unclean (Matt 15:1–20 = Mark 7:1–23).[18] Both forms of the pericope are composite. There are actually three issues here: the Pharisaic rules of cleanliness, the Korban vow (both of these bearing on the oral law), and the authority of the written law of the unclean. Matthew's form seems superficially more smooth, but Mark is actually more consistent, for 7:1–13 concerns the oral tradition and 7:15–23 the biblical law.

Mark's story is in three scenes. In the first, Jesus' disciples are criticized for not washing their hands, and this is answered by an attack on the oral tradition in which the vow ("Korban" in Mark) is given as a polemical argument. Mark places the Isaiah quotation before the Korban example. Second, Jesus summons the crowd and teaches that it is only that which comes out of a human being that defiles (Matt 15:10–11 = Mark 7:14–15). In Mark the third scene (7:17–23) is distinct from the

---

17 Tuckett, *Griesbach Hypothesis*, 96–102.
18 Tuckett, *Griesbach Hypothesis*, 102–10.

others. Jesus goes into a house and teaches the disciples privately, but in Matt 15:12 there is no change of scene; the disciples approach Jesus, say that the Pharisees were offended, and Jesus answers (15:12–14). The answer implies that Jesus is attacking the oral law taught by "blind guides," but he has previously abrogated the priestly laws themselves. Peter then asks Jesus to explain the "parable" (15:15), but in Mark the disciples ask this when they enter the house, and in the explanation Mark adds a clause with a hanging participle "cleansing all foods."

If is curious that, if Mark had access to Matthew and Luke, he ignored a logion on the inside and the outside of the cup (Matt 23:25–26 = Luke 11:39–41) which would have served his purpose well in teaching that all foods are clean. Tuckett discusses this only in connection with the problem of the relative order of passages in Matthew and Luke.[19] In both gospels this saying has the Woe-form which, as we have seen, is characteristic of Q material but not of Mark. One can of course argue that Mark would have found the saying too obscure.[20]

When we consider Luke's special material, we have seen that he included the two stories of healing on the Sabbath which involve an argument of rabbinic type. Otherwise when he transmits an argument of halakhic type it has been derived from Matthew or (according to the 2DH) from Mark or Q. While Luke believed that Jesus taught the permanence of the law;[21] he was relatively uninterested in controversies over it. Such matters belonged to the past, and he was writing for a predominantly Gentile church. His point of view is well expressed by James' speech (Acts 15:19–21) and the decree of the council (15:28–29); cf. also 13:38. At the same time he had a special reverence for the Temple as the place where Jesus was presented to God and where he and the apostles taught, even though in his time it had been destroyed.[22]

It is understandable, therefore, that if Luke used Matthew, he rewrote the great Sermon by omitting the antitheses of 5:21–24, 33–37

---

[19] Tuckett, *Griesbach Hypothesis*, 30–40.

[20] Luke's wording, "Give alms with respect to what is inside," makes no sense. The mention of alms obscures the point that the purity laws are abolished. Mark therefore would not have used Luke's form, though he favored almsgiving (12:41–44). Matthew's form, "Cleanse first the inside of the cup," fits the argument. It seems inconceivable that Luke should have copied Matthew at this point.

[21] J. D. Kingsbury, *Jesus Christ in Matthew, Mark, and Luke* (Philadelphia: Fortress, 1981) 116–18.

[22] Cf. J. B. Tyson, "Scripture, Torah and Sabbath in Luke-Acts," in *Jesus, the Gospels and the Church* (ed. E. P. Sanders; Macon, GA: Mercer University Press, 1987) 84–104. Tyson sees both continuity and discontinuity in Luke's view of Torah.

and transferring some other parts of Matthew's Sermon to other places in his gospel. The result is that the Sermon on the Plain is entirely kerygmatic and paraenetic and concerns love, non-resistance, and generosity. The antithetic form "You have heard that is was said..." is not present. But Luke's Sermon shows independence of Matthew, and the 2DH may be more persuasive here.

Where, now, does Mark stand with respect to the law, as compared with the other gospels? We consider this question first in the light of the GH. His gospel appears obviously more Hellenistic than that of Matthew, although at times, as when he uses the word *Korban*, he appears to have independent knowledge of Judaism. He can use arguments of rabbinic type, but does not do so as frequently as Matthew, and Jesus has an authority over the law which is sovereign and independent (2:10, 3:4, 7:14–15). Mark thinks of the disciples as going on a mission wearing sandals (6:9) and this may imply a long journey, perhaps outside Palestine. He also applies the divorce saying to what may be a Gentile situation (10:12).

If Mark has access to Matthew's divorce logion, he rejects or ignores the exception clause. This could be ascribed to an ascetical tendency— Hermas who reflects rather little gospel material, condemns marriage after divorce (*Mand* 4:1,6)—but Mark, unlike Matthew (19:10–12), does not have to justify asceticism. He also ignores the special authority committed to Peter and the Church (Matt 16:19, 18:15–20). If he is opposed to a religion of glory and success, he may also deny that the leaders of the Church have authority to legislate. This could be an implicit protest against the institutional development of the Church.

Is Luke's gospel more Hellenistic than that of Mark? Both belong to the Hellenistic Church, Luke most obviously. But it is a question of nuances. Luke has a veneration for the law that Mark does not exhibit, but it seems retrospective, explaining Jesus' setting in Jewish history, rather than a positive propaganda in favor of the law. In Acts he goes so far as to say that there were Pharisees among Jerusalem Christians and that Paul claimed to be a Pharisee; but the law, except for the provision of Acts 15:28–29, is not binding on Gentiles. In this respect, Mark appears to be more radical than Luke; and yet Mark gives the impression of writing for a church (possibly Rome) which is in close contact with a Jewish community,[23] and needs to defend itself. Luke defends the gospel in a different way.

Historical study sometimes has to work with nuances that are subtle, and how one views the setting of Mark with respect to the law depends partly on what one finds most appropriate and likely. Here the literary phenomena may be more important than an attempt to assess the overall picture.

Mark in Relation to Judaism and Hellenism

Is it possible to determine where each of the gospels stands in relation to Judaism and Hellenism? Long ago I remarked that Mark was written when "the Church is just at the point of emerging from Judaism as a new, self-conscious community."[24] The claims of the GH require that the question be raised again. At the present time scholars believe that there were various types of Jewish and Hellenistic Christianity. For example, Perrin mentions Palestinian Jewish Christianity, Hellenistic Jewish Mission Christianity, Gentile Christianity apart from Paul, and Pauline, Post-Pauline, and Johannine Christianity.[25] Raymond Brown has attempted a more precise analysis and distinguishes four basic types among Jewish Christians and their Gentile converts: (1) those who demanded full observance of the Mosaic law, including circumcision; (2) those who did not demand circumcision but required Gentiles to keep some Jewish observances, such as the food laws (Acts 15:20, Gal 2:12); (3) missionaries like Paul who did not insist on either circumcision or the food laws; (4) Christians like Paul who in addition saw no abiding significance in Jewish cult and fasts.[26]

From this point of view, the Fourth Gospel, like the Epistle to the Hebrews, belongs in the fourth group. It is not clear where Luke-Acts belongs, for the Gospel of Luke contains sayings on the permanence of the law, together with criticism of the lawyers and their interpretation. Acts, at least, records the decision in Jerusalem requiring kosher foods, but Stephen's speech is radical in its rejection of the Temple and its cultus

---

[23]   Cf. S. E. Johnson, *A Commentary on the Gospel according to St. Mark* (London: Black, 1977) 5–9, where I argued that Mark is a boundary gospel, in between Judaism and Hellenistic Christianity.

[24]   Johnson, *St. Mark*, 6.

[25]   N. Perrin and D. C. Duling, *The New Testament: An Introduction* (2nd ed.; New York: Harcourt Brace Jovanovich, 1982) 73–81.

[26]   R. E. Brown and J. P. Meier, *Antioch and Rome* (New York: Paulist Press, 1983) 2–9.

(7:44–53). Luke himself may have wished to take an irenic position and to tolerate differences of opinion and practice, but Paul's final speech in Acts 28:25b–28 reflects despair over the conversion of large numbers of Jews; the Church's destiny is with the Gentiles.

Matthew and Mark should perhaps be placed in the third group; Matthew shows relatively more sympathy with the Jewish tradition. Mark much less. This observation gives no help in assessing the GH, but it tends to put Mark in the middle position between Matthew and Luke.

Farmer takes the position that a tradition which does not reflect a Palestinian or Jewish setting is secondary to one which does so. Tuckett answers that the greater Jewishness of Matthew may be due merely to the fact that Matthew's readers were better acquainted with Judaism than were those of Mark.[27] It is now widely believed that Matthew wrote for congregations that were in close proximity to the revived Pharisaism which began with Johanan ben Zakkai. Antioch is indeed a logical place for such churches,[28] but Palestine itself cannot be excluded. If Mark was written in Rome, the Jewish community there may not have been in close touch with this Pharisaic revival; if by any chance the gospel was written in Galilee, the Christians there may not yet have been affected by it.

Study of Semitisms and Latinisms in the gospels does not add much to our knowledge of Mark's cultural setting; it simply confirms what we know from other traits of his gospel, that his tradition is in touch with Judaism and Hellenism.

The large number of Aramaic (3:17, 5:41, 7:34, 10:51, 15:34) and Hebrew (7:11, 9:5, 11:21, 14:45) words in Mark, most of which are not found in the parallel passages, is a phenomenon that has been debated. Only the "Rabbi" in 14:45 is found in a Matthaean parallel (26:49). "Rabbi" in 9:5 corresponds to κύριε (Matt 17:4) and ἐπιστάτα (Luke 9:33). The Aramaic "Rabbouni" (10:51; cf. John 20:16) is reflected by κύριε in Matt 20:33 and Luke 18:41. Whereas in Mark 15:34, Jesus on the Cross cries out *Eloi, Eloi* (Aramaic), Matt 27:46 has the Hebrew *Eli, Eli*.

Matthew does, however, sometimes introduce such words. In Matt 26:25, Judas asks, μήτι ἐγώ εἰμι, ῥαββί; in Mark 14:19 each of the disciples say μήτι ἐγώ. The disciples are told in Matt 23:7 that they are not to be called Rabbi. Matt 5:22 contains the word ῥαχά and μαμωνᾶ is found in Matt 6:24; Luke 16:9, 11, 13.

---

27   Tuckett, *Griesbach Hypothesis*, 10–11, 103–10.
28   W. R. Farmer, *Jesus and the Gospel* (Philadelphia: Fortress, 1982) 135–38.

Matthew Black finds traces of Aramaic locutions in Mark, but they are also common in the other gospels, so that an Aramaism is not in itself significant. But there is one Aramaic peculiarly, ἀπέχει, in Mark 14:41, which is not paralleled in Matthew or Luke.[29]

If, as the GH would suggest, the frequency of Semitisms is due to Mark's editing of Matthew and Luke, the only reason is that of any historical novelist, to tell a better story. These cases are not necessarily editorial in character. If any of them are, one could say that Matt 26:25 makes an editorial change, inserting "Rabbi" in the editing of Mark 14:19 and attributing the question to Judas. One might argue, on the other hand, that Mark has made the change in order to show that all the disciples had an uneasy conscience.

Latin words and Latinisms are not necessarily significant; those in the gospels are attested in papyri, inscriptions, Hellenistic writers, and sometimes in rabbinic literature. They were likely to occur anywhere in the empire. This is especially true of πραιτώριον (Mark 15:16 = Matt 27:27; not in the Lucan parallel). Other words shared by Mark and Matthew are φραγελλόω (Mark 15:15 = Matt 27:26), κῆνσος (Mark 12:14 = Matt 22:17); Luke 20:22 has φόρος (cf. Matt 17:25), and κοδράντης (Mark 12:42; not in parallels to this verse but in Matt 5:20 = Luke 12:59).

Mark has one Latinism, ποιῆσαι τὸ ἱκανόν (= *satis facere*, 15:15), which is not represented in the parallels. Another, συμβούλιον ἐποίησαν (Mark 3:6) or συμβούλιον ποιήσαντες (15:1) has variants in both verses, but in each case the reading has good attestation.

Mark also has two Latin words not attested in parallels, σπεκουλάτωρ (6:27) and κεντυρίων (15:39, 44, 45). Matthew and Luke use the Greek equivalent for the latter (Matt 27:54 = Luke 23:47; Matt 8:5, 8 = Luke 7:2, 6 cf. Acts 10:1; 27:1, 31).

The net result is that Mark is somewhat more given to Latinism. This might be a colloquial trait.

There are numerous signs that Mark writes for a mainly Gentile church. What is most obvious is the way in which he builds up a kind of charter for the mission to Gentiles, beginning with the command to the Gerasene (5:19), continuing with the story of the Syrophoenician woman and the tour through heathen territory (7:24–30, 31–8:10), the proclamation that the Temple is a house of prayer for all nations (11:17), and finally the statement that the gospel must be preached to all the nations

---

[29] M. Black, *An Aramaic Approach to the Gospels and Acts* (3rd ed.; Oxford: Clarendon Press, 1967) 225–28.

(13:10). Matthew also teaches the universal mission in the eschatological chapter (24:14) and has suggested Jesus' concern for Gentiles in the stories of the centurion of Capharnaum and the Canaanite woman. Luke has developed the theme in his own way. In this respect there is little difference among the three gospels.

We have also seen that Mark adapts older traditions to a Gentile audience; the permission to wear sandals (6:9) can apply to journeys outside Palestine, though this may be fanciful. It contradicts Matt 10:10 and Luke 10:4. The clause in Mark looks like an awkward redactional addition, and this is in favor of the GH. Luke 9:3 says nothing about sandals. The presumption that a woman might divorce her husband (10:12) also suggests the Roman world.

Although Mark is evidently more Hellenistic than Matthew, there are Semitic and Palestinian features in this gospel. The oscillation between Jewish and Hellenistic elements may be due to Mark's redaction and the character of his sources. The oral character of Mark's speech is neither Hellenistic nor Semitic in itself; it is, however, important as an argument in favor of Mark's priority.

CHAPTER NINE

Selected Passages

Several passages that have a bearing on the GH call for detailed attention. The first of these has been claimed to reflect an overlap between Mark and Q. Supporters of the GH claim that the theory of an overlap weakens the 2DH.

The Beelzebul Controversy

The Beelzebul controversy in Mark 3:22–30 is framed by 3:20–21, in which Jesus is in a house surrounded by a crowd, whereupon οἱ παρ' αὐτοῦ (his family?) come to take him away, "for they said, 'he is beside himself,'" and the passage 3:31–35, in which Jesus says that the people with him in the house are his true family.

Matthew's parallel (12:24–32) is introduced by a brief incident in which Jesus heals a blind and dumb man and the crowds say, "Can this be the son of David?" (12:22–23). This in turn follows a summary of healings with a formula citation of Isa 42:1–4. Matthew follows 12:32 with several non-Marcan passages including sayings on the expulsion of demons (12:43–45 = Luke 11:24–26) and resumes the story of the visit of the family only at 12:46. Here the Beelzebul pericope is not framed; Mark 3:20–21 has no parallel in the other gospels.

Luke's form of the controversy is in 11:14–23; 12:10. This is in a very different context, after important passages on prayer (11:1–13), and is introduced by the brief account of Jesus' exorcism of a demon of dumbness which has some similarities to the introduction in Matt 12:22–23, but is much closer in wording to Matt 9:32–33 and is often assigned to Q. Luke thus has no counterpart to Mark 3:31–35 except for Luke 8:19–21, which comes at an earlier point in his narrative, after the parables discourse.

The 2DH practically demands that there be an overlap of Mark and Q. Although in general Q represents the "double tradition" in Matthew and Luke, there are sayings and pericopes, such as the parable of the Mustard-seed, in which Mark has one wording, while Matthew and Luke—and especially Luke—bear witness to a separate form.[1] Thus, the 2DH finds Mark 3:22–30 to be an independent pericope, and Matt 12:35–37 weaves this in with another pericope independent of it (Q) which is represented by Luke 11:17–23; 12:10.

Mark's account also contains some curious features. If he is using the other gospels he ignores the powerful argument that Jesus casts out demons by the Spirit (or finger) of God (Matt 12:27–28 = Luke 11:19–20), together with the statement that the Kingdom of God has arrived, and the saying, "Whoever is not with me is against me, and whoever does not gather with me scatters" (Matt 12:30 = Luke 11:23).[2] What is most curious is the statement in Mark 3:28–29. The parallel saying, Matt 12:31–32 (=Luke 12:10), more brief and in a different context, teaches that a word against the Son of Man can be forgiven, but not a blasphemy against the Holy Spirit. Mark appears to have recast this logion, whatever source he may have used: "Truly I tell you, all the sins and blasphemies will be forgiven the *sons of men*. . . but whoever blasphemes the Holy Spirit. . . is guilty of an eternal sin, because they were saying 'He has an unclean spirit.'" Such a charge against Jesus is the unforgivable sin.[3] This in itself tends to support the GH, but if Mark is editing Matthew and Luke, he has taken pains to produce what has been called a mostly "Q-free" pericope by omitting Matt 12:27–28 = Luke 11:19–20.

---

[1] Cf. C. M. Tuckett, *The Revival of the Griesbach Hypothesis: An Analysis and Appraisal* (Cambridge: Cambridge University Press, 1985) 85–89; A. D. Jacobson, "The Literary Unity of Q," *JBL* 101 (1982) 381. D. Lührmann, "The Gospel of Mark and the Sayings Collection Q," *JBL* 108 (1989) 62-63, discusses passages common to Mark and Q. The Beelzebul controversy and the demand for a sign are in sequence in Luke 11:14–26, 29–32 and Matt 12:22–30, 39–45. In my opinion, each of the two evangelists inserts a different pericope between the two parts. Neither of these probably stood in Q at this point. Matt 12:33–35 is a doublet of 7:16–20 in the Sermon on the Mount, which has a corresponding parallel in Luke 6:43–45.

[2] Formally this contradicts the saying about the exorcist, Mark 9:40 = Luke 9:50, but the situations are different. In each case the question is, Who is on Jesus' side?

[3] Elsewhere Mark mentions the Holy Spirit rather seldom, 1:8, 10, 12; 12:36 (David speaking in a Psalm); 13:11. Jesus perceives in his spirit the thoughts of the critics (2:8). The peculiarity of Mark 3:28–29 may be significant and anticipated by 1:10.

The Storm at Sea

The tempest on the lake is the first nature miracle in Mark (4:35–41), as it is in Matthew (8:23–27). Luke, however, has already told of a miraculous catch of fish. Of the three, Mark gives the story in the greatest detail. Luke's account (8:22–25) follows that of Mark in the main, while Matthew is significantly different. Bornkamm regards this as an example of Matthew's adaptation of traditional material to the situation of the Church in his day. The Church is symbolized by the disciples in the boat; it is tossed about in a hostile world. Chapter 8 comes just after the Sermon on the Mount; the context of this pericope is discipleship, and the key word is "follow" (8:18–22). The rebuke to the disciples appears *before* Jesus stills the storm, because they already recognize his divine nature (as I have noted in Chapter 7) and therefore they cry out, "Lord, save; we are perishing!" It is true that in Mark 4:38 the disciples believe that Jesus has some power, but there they merely say, "Teacher, don't you care. . .?" Matthew, says Bornkamm, is the oldest exegete of the Marcan narrative.[4]

Like many other redaction critics, Bornkamm assumes the 2DH. If we consider the GH here, it is necessary to see what Mark has apparently done. (1) Both Matthew and Mark have εἰς τὸ πέραν, which is a favorite phrase of Mark, and other Marcan traits appear in this pericope.[5] (2) Mark, however, has produced a more wordy and vivid narrative. Jesus is asleep on a cushion in the stern. The word λαῖλαψ is used. Most curiously, Mark mentions the presence of other boats, and there is no reason why he should do so unless it is in his source. Some similarly unmotivated boats appear in John 6:22, and this suggests that some oral tradition lies behind Mark's account and John's story of the walking on the water and its sequel. (4) In Matthew's pericope, καὶ ἐμβάντι αὐτῷ (8:23) and ὀλιγόπιστοι (8:26) seem to be marks of that evangelist's style.

It can be argued that Mark does not have Jesus criticize the disciples prior to the stilling of the storm because he is building up the motif of their unbelief gradually. This would fit with his general point of view. A severe criticism is more appropriate after the later story of Jesus walking on the water. Otherwise, a comparison of Matthew and Mark at this point does not support the GH.

---

4 G. Bornkamm, G. Barth, and H.-J. Held, *Tradition and Interpretation in Matthew* (Philadelphia: Westminster, 1963) 52–57.

5 D. B. Peabody, *Mark as Composer* (Macon, GA: Mercer University Press, 1987) 76–77 (Tables 123, 124, 126–30).

The Gerasene Demoniac

In all three gospels the account of the storm on the lake precedes that of the wild maniac in the tombs (Mark 5:1–20 = Matt 8:28–34 = Luke 8:26–39), and in Mark and Luke the healings of Jaïrus' daughter and the woman with the haemorrhage are the next item. Matthew, however, inserted parallels to Mark 2:1–22 prior to the latter miracles.

The three gospels agree that the exorcism occurs on the "other side," the east or pagan side of the lake. On this occasion, according to Mark and Luke, Jesus departs from his usual practice of forbidding mention of the healing, for he tells the man who is restored to sanity to go to his own people and report to them how many things the Lord (the true God) has done for him. This is the only time when Jesus is in pagan territory prior to Mark 7:21. (Luke never again indicates that Jesus is in a Gentile region, for he does not specify the location of Peter's confession.)

Matthew's story is much more brief, Luke is more detailed, and Mark has the longest form of all. The GH would demand that Luke has built up the pericope in Matthew with a longer account, changing "Gadarenes" to "Gerasenes" or possibly "Gergesenes," substituting for Matthew's two men a single wild maniac possessed by the Legion, and adding Jesus' order to the man to return to his home. Mark, in turn, has changed the order of Luke by describing at an earlier point how the man had been chained and fettered (5:4–5). He would also have substituted ὁ κύριος (5:29) for ὁ θεός (Luke 8:39). Luke and Mark have also omitted πρὸ καιροῦ in Matt 8:29 ("why have you come to torment us before the time?")[6]

Here I find the 2DH more satisfactory. "Gadarenes" could easily be a correction; and Matthew tends to double the actors in a story (cf. 9:27, 20:30).

Caesarea Philippi

In Chapter 1 I have discussed the difficulty of sustaining the GH in the Caesarea Philippi pericope (Matt 16:14–28). It may be added that in Matthew the doctrine of the Church is more developed than in the other

---

[6] The phrase in Matthew reflects a doctrine, attested in Enoch, Jubilees, and the Testament of Levi, that demonic activity will cease only at the end of the age. In Mark and Luke, furthermore, the demons, instead of addressing Jesus merely as Son of God, say "Son of the Most High," a phrase appropriate in the mouth of a Gentile. 5:1–2 is an introduction very much in Mark's style, but the same traits appear also in the parallel, Matt 8:28.

Synoptics. The new Christian community is in continuity with the old religion but is distinct from contemporary Judaism in being the true Israel. Matthew should now be compared with Luke and Mark with respect to the self-consciousness of the community.

Of the four gospels, that of Matthew is the only one to use the word ἐκκλησία. This can correspond to the *qahal* of the OT, the sacred congregation of Israel, but also to *keneseth* (Aram. *kenishta*), a congregation of synagogue. Even if this is a community of eschatological expectation, the fact is that it receives special emphasis.

Jesus promises Peter that he will be the rock on which the Church is to be built (Matt 16:16). Perhaps this reference is to a church that will come only after the Resurrection. Nevertheless, there is a rule in 18:15–17 which provides that the final settlement of a grievance is to be made by the Church, which in extreme cases has the power of excommunication. Here "church" is evidently the local congregation. This is certainly legislation applying to the time when Matthew writes, and the evangelist appends sayings teaching that the decision will be ratified in heaven and that where two or three are gathered in Jesus' name he is present in their midst (18:18–20). "Binding and loosing" there has become more than the rabbinic authority to declare something forbidden or permitted, which is probably the meaning in 16:19.[7]

We have noted that the Son of Man has a kingdom in Matthew, but this may be eschatological (13:41–42, 16:28). The Son of Man will finally judge all the nations (25:31–46). But although his Parousia is yet to come, the risen Christ already has all authority in heaven and earth; the Eleven are to make disciples of all nations, baptize and preach, and he is with them till the end of the age (28:18–21).

The Gospel of Luke makes no mention of any church as such; there are disciples of Jesus—the Twelve, the Seventy-two, and others, both men and women. The risen Christ commissions the Eleven to be witnesses to all nations (24:46–49; cf. Acts 1:4–5). At Pentecost they are endowed with the Spirit (Acts 2:1–3) and about three thousand people are added to this missionary movement (2:41) and are being saved (2:47). The movement as a whole is sometimes called "the Way" (9:2; 19:9, 23; 22:4; 24:14, 22; cf. "the way of the Lord," 18:25; "the way of God," 18:26).

When Acts uses the word ἐκκλησία, as it does at least twenty-three times, it preserves the general meaning of "assembly," which can be observed in 19:32, 39, 41 (the mob in the theater of Ephesus). Most often it

---

7 Cf. pp. 94, 96–97, 119, 139, and note 11 to Chap. 8.

designates a specific congregation in Jerusalem (e.g., 5:11, 8:1, 11:22), Antioch (13:1, 14:27), or Caesarea (18:22). Paul appoints presbyters in every church (14:23). There are a few places where "church" may denote a wider region (9:31, all Judaea; possibly 15:22, 20:28), and in one passage the church in the desert refers to the sacred congregation of Israel (9:31). Luke is concerned for the unity of Christians, but he never expresses clearly Paul's concept of the Church as universal and realized concretely in local churches.

The Gospel of Mark uses the Pauline word εὐαγγέλιον, as the other gospels do, but not Paul's important word ἐκκλησία. There is no thought of the Church as the Body of Christ or the concept of being "in Christ Jesus," and there is only the one example of belonging to Christ (9:41). If Mark has a concept of a church, he expresses it through the symbol of the crowd (ὄχλος)[8] that listens to Jesus; the word is used in an unfavorable sense only in 15:8, 11, 15. One possible hint of the Church as a separate entity is found in the story of the exorcist (9:38–40), though here the disciples are the group to which he does not belong.

Mark's gospel is less ecclesiastical, but this is not because he deliberately omits the passages in Matt 16 and 18. The band of disciples and hearers that is reflected in Mark is apart from the main stream of Judaism, but is essentially a group that awaits the Son of Man, the end of the present age, and establishment of the Reign of God.

The gospel does reflect a probability that there are conflicts of authority in the existing Church. These could occur at any time from the days of Paul's ministry through the early 2nd century (or later), as the criticism of Jesus' brothers in John 7:3–5 suggests. Followers of the original Twelve, members of the Lord's family, and other groups may have been in competition here and there. The evidence therefore gives no clear help in determining the setting of Mark, except that the gospel makes Galilee the symbolic place of true Christianity.

Introduction to the Feeding of the Five Thousand

There are a few pericopes in Mark which might support the GH or are at least neutral with regard to the two hypotheses. One of these is Mark's elaborate introduction to the Feeding of the Five Thousand (6:30–34; cf. Matt 14:10–14 and Luke 9:10–11, which is more brief). In Mark,

---

8 P. S. Minear, "Audience Criticism and Markan Eschatology," in *Neues Testament und Geschichte* (ed. H. Bartelsweiler and B. Reicke; Zürich and Tübingen: Gotthelf, 1972) 79–89.

Jesus has compassion on the crowds, which are like sheep without a shepherd, and he "began to teach them many things;" Matthew says that he healed the sick among them.

The solution of the 2DH should be that Matthew and Luke were not interested in Mark's emphasis on teaching at this point, or in the OT allusion to sheep without a shepherd, which together with the hundreds and fifties of 6:40 suggested the presence of an army. Luke, however, states that Jesus taught the crowds about the Reign of God (a characteristically Lucan touch) and also healed. Thus it could be argued in support of the GH that Luke derived the mention of healings from Matthew. Mark then picked up Luke's note about Jesus' teaching and combined it with other elements in his introduction because of his desire to show that the miracles were always connected with Jesus' teaching, indeed that he taught through these wonders.

The Names of the Disciples

The traditions regarding the names of the Twelve (or of Jesus' intimate disciples) are in only partial agreement.

It is curious that in Mark 2:14 and Luke 5:27 the disciple who is enlisted as he sits at the tax office is named Levi, while in Matt 9:9 it is Matthew (cf. Matt 10:3, "Matthew the tax collector"). The solution of the GH is that Luke has changed the name but there is no easily discernible reason for this. If we reason from the 2DH, we suppose that Matthew has changed the name because later he will refer to Matthew as the tax collector. There is, further, a peculiarity in Mark's text (2:14); James is substituted for Levi in some MSS usually assigned to the Caesarean and Western text types. In Matthew's list, James the son of Alphaeus immediately follows Matthew, and it is possible that ὁ τελώνης was originally attached to James, but came to be connected to Matthew instead.[9]

An examination of the order of names in the lists of the Twelve in the Synoptics and the Eleven in Acts is, otherwise, of no help in determining the relationships of the gospels. The lists consist of three groups of four each. In Group I the same four names occur throughout, and Matthew and Luke have the same order. Mark and Acts make Andrew the fourth, but Acts differs from the gospels in placing John ahead of James. Group II agrees on four names, and Mark and Luke have the same order. In Group III, James son of Alphaeus is first, and Judas Iscariot last. Simon the Zealot is second in Luke and Acts, but Simon the Cananaean is third

---

[9] B. W. Bacon, *Studies in Matthew* (New York: Henry Holt, 1930) 39–40.

in Matthew and Mark. The remaining figure is problematical. The UBS text reads Thaddaeus in both Matthew and Mark, but there is evidence, mostly western, for Lebbaeus in both these gospels. In Luke and Acts it is Judas of James.

The phenomena could be accounted for by the GH or by the 2DH. In the case of the former, Mark seems to have skipped back and forth between Matthew and Luke, but not consistently. My guess is that each of the Synoptists had a list which he knew by memory and none of them copied another gospel.

The Mission Charges

As we have seen previously, there are passages in which the hypothesis of Q seems to be the most probable solution. For example, the GH almost requires that in composing the parable of the Mustard-seed, Mark was determined to produce a "Q-free" or Luke-free pericope.[10]

When one compares the mission of the Seventy-two (Luke 10:1–12) with the parallels, Matt 9:37–38, 10:7–16, Mark 6:6–13 and Luke 9:1–6, it appears that if one of these pericopes is theologically more primitive than the other, it is surely Luke 10:1–16. Unless this is a Q passage, the most likely solution is that Luke has a special source at this point. The only alternative would seem to be that he has performed a *tour de force* by abstracting materials from Matt 9:37–10:16, and then adding 10:13–16 (=Matt 11:21–23, 10:40) in such a way as to produce an apparently more primitive form of a mission discourse or proclamation of the Reign of God and judgment.

Defense of Q, however, rests on much more; for example, the form-critical differences between Mark and the Q material, to which Jacobson has called attention, and the fact that in Mark, Jesus is not the eschatological judge.[11]

---

10   Cf. pp. 88–89.
11   Cf. pp. 111.

CHAPTER TEN

Conclusion

I

This study has observed two types of compositional phenomena. The first is literary and stylistic. Farmer's arguments for the GH concentrate on this, and so do his colleagues and such critics as Talbert, McKnight and Tuckett. The results of the latter seem persuasive to me. Then there are many features in the Synoptics which are theological in the broadest sense; i.e., some of these concern the sociological and cultural setting of the gospels. It is these which in my opinion have not hitherto been sufficiently taken into account. In many pericopes the two types of phenomena are combined, and here the results are of great importance.

In some cases the traits of composition can be used to support the GH. I observe, however, that many of these are "neutral," i.e., the solution offered by the 2DH is equally good or preferable. Therefore I conclude that the latter still stands as the best solution of the Synoptic problem that research has presented.

II

Literary and Stylistic

Mark's style is in the direction of the oral and colloquial. His frequent roughness and naïveté suggest that often he depends upon oral tradition, and that the smoother language of Matthew and Luke in the parallels is due to their rewriting. Matthew's characteristic stylistic traits are often very visible in this redaction, and to some degree this is also true of Luke.

Mark was not "writing down" to his readers—it was not like a situation in which the NT is translated into Basic English, for the same readers would have had no difficulty understanding Matthew and Luke, and Mark used hypotaxis when he chose to do so—it is rather that his style was natural to him. Furthermore, many would regard his reflections of Palestinian life (in 2:1 the men dig through the roof) as a sign of the primitive character of his gospel.

The fact that the woe-form is almost completely lacking in Mark, together with other features of the so-called Q material, argues in favor of the 2DH and the existence of Q.

Unless Achtemeier's discovery, namely that two catenae of miracles lie behind Mark, is a delusion, Mark is prior to the other gospels at this point.

Several specific pericopes in Mark force me to the same conclusion: the Korban vow, 7:1–23; the Herodians and Herod in 3:6, 8:15, 12:13; the divorce passage, 10:2–12; the healings of blind, deaf and dumb men, especially 10:46–52; Matthew's substitution of *Eli, Eli* for *Eloi, Eloi* in 27:46 (cf. Mark 15:34); and the empty tomb, 16:1–8.[1]

III

Theological and Cultural

The shapes or basic structures of the three gospels persuade me to favor the 2DH. Mark has built his gospel in such a way that the latter part is often anticipated by hints in 1:1—8:26, and there is a definite strategy by which he progressively teaches that Jesus is Son of God and Son of Man. It is difficult for me to suppose that he has abstracted elements from Matthew in order to achieve this. This is seen especially when the Christologies of the three gospels are compared.

Something like the divine man theology is present in all three Synoptics, but expressed by each of the evangelists in his own way. This in itself has no bearing on the Synoptic problem unless, for example, Luke heightens a tendency found in Mark.

Mark is unusual in reflecting what can be read as an adoptionist Christology which, if it is not primitive, must be a revision. The Christologies of Matthew and Luke are homogeneous in the sense that they are syntheses of various approaches to the understanding of Jesus' nature. Mark, however, plays down the concept of Messiah, reinterprets

---

[1] See pp. 38–39.

it, and apparently rejects the son of David aspect of it. The Son of Man sayings are fitted into the gospel in such a way as to prepare for an announcement of Jesus' suffering, death, and resurrection as Son of Man. The Son of Man does not have a kingdom of his own, but his return to Galilee is the expected climax of history, and even the resurrection is subordinated to this. When the Son of Man will arrive, there is no hint that he will be eschatological judge. It is said only that he will gather the elect (Mark 13:27).

The other great theme is the Reign of God. Most interpretations of Mark understand this as entirely a future event; e.g., Mark does not have the logion Matt 12:28 = Luke 11:20. If, however, Kelber's reading of the gospel is correct, Mark affirms that presence of the Kingdom, though not its consummation, in a unique manner.[2] Such an interpretation of the Kingdom would be difficult to derive from Matthew and Luke.

There is little trace of the Gehenna/Heaven eschatology in Mark. It is represented better in Matthew and Luke.

Mark's treatment of Torah is not as developed as it is in the other gospels, although at times he shows knowledge of Jewish rules and customs. In general he rejects the old law more radically than do Matthew and Luke. The OT has authority, but the supreme authority is Jesus.

Matthew's promises to Peter and the Church (16:18–19, 18:15–20), which reflect a marked development of ecclesiology, must always be a difficulty for the GH, which presumes that Mark ignores this feature totally.

It is easier to suppose that Matthew and Luke have softened Mark's criticism of the Twelve and the Lord's family than that Mark has sharpened it. Here the discourse on the loaves (Mark 8:14–21; cf. Matt 16:1–4) and 6:52, which prepares for it, are crucially important. The difference between 4:35–41 and Matt 8:23–29 (the storm at sea) may also be significant with respect to the treatment of the disciples in the two gospels. If, however, Mark is dependent on Matthew and Luke, he deliberately modifies these passages to reject the authority of those whom most Christians regarded as the Church's original leaders. The only people therefore to be followed are those who seek no preëminence for themselves and who follow the way of the Cross and the Son of Man who made himself servant and slave of all (Mark 10:45). Yet the way of the Cross is not absent in the other gospels. If Mark has used them and is sharpening the point, it gives the impression of a return to Paul's insight

---

2 See p. 81.

into the gospel. Mark, of course, discloses no knowledge of Paul's letters. In the post-apostolic age no Christian writer who honored Paul was a "Paulinist" in the sense that Mark may be considered one, with the possible and partial exception of Luke and Ignatius, certainly not the authors of the Pastoral Epistles and First Clement. And Mark is not like Marcion.

IV

Theological and Stylistic Traits Combined

The remarks previously made about the shape of the gospels also indicate differences in the compositional habits of the evangelist. Talbert has discerned some inner structures in Luke and has shown that in many cases they are to be explained by his editing of Mark.[3] I have argued that Mark has a more or less consistent topographical outline which he could not have borrowed from Matthew. In particular, Mark 8:22–26 begins a pattern of blindness and sight which is absent from the other gospels.

A number of pericopes in Mark exhibit features both compositional and theological, and here I regard Mark as primary. The evidence is cumulative. These passages include the plucking of grain on the sabbath (2:23–28), the man with the withered hand (3:1–6), the Beelzebul controversy (3:20–30), Caesarea Philippi (8:27–9:1), the dispute over rank (9:33–37), the sons of Zebedee (10:35–45), and especially the eschatological discourse (Chap. 13).

V

Neutral Features

The observation that Mark 1:1–15 can be understood as an abbreviation of Matt 3:1–4:13 is one of the more attractive features of the GH. This has always caused difficulty for the 2DH, and no doubt in modern times, as in ancient, has first led to the hypothesis that Matthew is the earliest gospel. Against it may be set the composition of Matt 8–9.[4]

Several other phenomena may be at least neutral as respects the two hypotheses. For example, an examination of Semitisms and Latinisms and various Jewish and Hellenistic cultural traits does not lead to a certain conclusion. Luke could have changed Matthew's "Kingdom of the

---

[3] See pp. 58–60, 65.
[4] See pp. 11, 14, 44–45.

heavens" to "Kingdom of God," which was already a standard phrase, whereupon Mark followed his lead. Both gospels might have ignored Matthew's formula citations of OT passages. In this case, Mark also ignored the typology and promise-fulfilment patterns of the other two, although he preserved some typology relating to Moses, Elijah and Elisha. He would have preferred Matthew's geography to that of Luke, although it must be said that his crossings of the lake are generally more consistent.

There are other pericopes in which I find the evidence balanced, e.g., the names of the disciples (Mark 2:13–14, 3:13–19 and parallels); the rejection of Jesus at home (6:1–6a); and the introduction to the feeding of the Five Thousand (6:30–34).

IV

The Limitations of Literary Analysis

Since we work with written documents, we have to use literary methods as far as they will take us. Source criticism, form criticism, and redaction criticism have proved to be essential tools for reconstructing the story of Jesus and of primitive Christianity. But there are variables that make many conclusions tentative. We do not know just how a later evangelist would rewrite an earlier gospel. Did he have the convenience of a codex or did he have to unroll a scroll from time to time? And did he always look at a written text or might he sometimes have depended on his memory of it? There is the possibility, too, that at some points he depended on an oral tradition known to him.[5]

---

[5] P. J. Achtemeier, "*Omne verbum sonat*: The New Testament and the Oral Environment of Late Western Antiquity," *JBL* 109 (1990) 3–27, now gives an answer to some of these questions. Not only did people read aloud, as in Acts 8:30; when they composed, if they did not dictate to a scribe, they spoke aloud as they were writing; "no writing occurred that was not vocalized" (15–16). In writing a book it was necessary to use verbal clues, as in orations, so that hearers could follow the structure of an argument (19–20). This requires us to revise our approach to identification of sources, for such a phrase as καὶ ἔλεγον αὐτοῖς might not mark a different source but be only a help to the hearers (21–26). I would, however, contend that there must be exception to this rule, for in Luke 17:20–21 a Reign of God saying is followed by a Son of Man saying (17:22–30). Achtemeier agrees that writers were most likely to quote from memory and felt free to alter what they "quoted" (27). So far as I know we have no evidence of a codex earlier than the famous Ryland papyrus of parts of John 18, which is usually dated in the first half of the 2nd century. Thus the earliest gospel MSS may have been on scrolls.

Edward Simons in 1880 propounded the theory that Luke used Mark and Lambda (=Q) with only a secondary use of Matthew. This is now the position of Robert Morgenthaler. In his major statistical study he discusses the minor agreements of Matthew and Luke in vocabulary, order of sentences and order of pericopes, and concludes that the use of Matthew in these instances does not remove the likelihood that Q and Mark are his principal sources.[6]

There is, of course, the further question whether Luke is actually later than Matthew, because the latter reflects a higher development of institutional life. But this may be due to differences in ecclesiology in the places where the gospels were written.

Another theory, that of Pierson Parker, which perhaps has not received sufficient attention, has not been discussed here. It might be interesting to test it by use of the method I have attempted to develop here.[7]

Reputable scholars also remind us that the Synoptic problem may be more complicated than the two (or four) source hypothesis or the GH presuppose. The subtle analysis of Boismard and Benoit may be liable to the charge that it involves too many unknown quantities (this is the

---

[6]   R. Morgenthaler, *Statistische Synopse* (Zürich and Stuttgart: Gotthelf, 1971) 300–305. I am indebted to Prof. Hobbs for calling this work to my attention and providing me with a copy of his own article. Toward the end of his discussion, Morgenthaler (312, n. 197) notes the appearance of works on the Q problem, including that of Polag, while his book was in press. These make it obvious, he says, that the Synoptic problem has not yet been solved and that the discussion is still in flux.

[7]   Pierson Parker, in *The Gospel before Mark* (Chicago: University of Chicago Press, 1953), claimed to have isolated a Proto-Matthew (K) which Matthew used along with Proto-Luke. Mark used K, and in turn Luke used Mark and Proto-Luke. In his article, "A Second Look at *The Gospel before Mark,*" JBL 100 (1981) 389–413, he develops his arguments further. Instead of Q he prefers the hypothesis of a Proto-Luke, which is well represented in the canonical Luke and not so well in Matthew. "Q" he maintains, represents merely those portions of Proto-Luke which were adopted by the final redactor of Matthew. Q merges well into the rest of Luke's gospel, but far less well into Matthew (408–11). This, of course, would make it impossible for Luke to have used canonical Matthew. K, the original Jewish-Christian gospel, contained the most Judaic elements, the prohibition of a mission to Gentiles, and the formula citations. The final redactor of Matthew was responsible for the gospel's high Christology, the doctrine of the Church in Chaps. 16 and 18, the mission to all nations and the idea that the Kingdom embraces all of Jesus' followers. This would explain many inconsistencies in canonical Matthew. Finally, Parker gives elaborate arguments for the lateness of Mark (389–405). Many of his points can be answered, but he argues that the bulk of them remains, i.e., they are cumulative. My answer to this is that the arguments for the 2DH, as opposed to the GH, are likewise cumulative.

principle of Occam's razor), but such a theory of multiple sources cannot be ruled out absolutely.[8]

VII

The Place of Mark in Early Christianity

Farmer and others have suggested that Mark produced an irenic or neutral gospel to avoid apparent contradictions between Matthew and Luke.[9] But Mark's treatment of the Twelve and Jesus' family is anything but irenic.

Farmer also makes the reasonable suggestion that because the Passion story is so prominent, one purpose of Mark was liturgical.[10] The Christian Passover would be a logical time for reading the Passion narrative. The first document that gives much insight into such a celebration is Melito's *Homily on the Passover* in the late 2nd century. How the gospels were used liturgically in such a setting, and what scriptures (except for the Passion story) were read along with Melito's highly typological sermon we can only guess. Matthew's gospel especially divides easily into pericopes for public reading.[11]

If Mark derived most of his material from Matthew and Luke, one ought to remember that in that case Mark and John belong together in a late phase of the post-apostolic period. This is a matter of relative rather than of absolute dating, but it means also that Matthew and Luke must be dated as early as possible. The result of such a scenario is that the two gospels which contain large amounts of Jesus' teaching, and have the characteristics of sacred history, are followed by the two most keryg-

---

[8] P. Benoit and M. E. Boismard, *Synopse des quatre évangiles en français avec parallèles des apocryphes et des Pères*. 1 (Paris: Cerf, 1965); 2 *Commentaires* (1972). This is discussed by F. W. Beare, "On the Synoptic Problem: A New Documentary Theory," in *ATR* Supplementary Series 3 (1974) 15–28.

[9] W. R. Farmer, "Modern Developments of Griesbach's Hypothesis," *NTS* 23 (1977) 275–95; D. L. Dungan, "Reactionary Trends in the Gospel Producing Activity in the Early Church; Marcion, Tatian, Mark," in *L'Évangile selon Marc, Tradition et Rédaction* (ed. M. Sabbe; Leuven: Leuven University Press, 1988) 179–202.

[10] Farmer, *Synoptic Problem*, 279.

[11] Philip Carrington, *The Primitive Christian Calendar* (Cambridge: Cambridge University Press, 1952), developed the theory that Mark was composed as a series of liturgical pericopes, with the Passion narrative as a Passover reading. M. H. Shepherd, Jr., *The Paschal Liturgy and the Apocalypse* (Richmond: John Knox Press, 1960), compares the structure of the Book of Revelation with the first part of the Greek liturgy.

matic gospels, one of which has an independent story line and is highly developed theologically while the other gives the impression of primitivity. The trajectory method of Robinson and Koester puts the Fourth Gospel late in a complicated development,[12] and one asks how we may construct a trajectory into which Mark can be fitted.

We do not know as much as we should like about Christianity at the end of the 2nd century and the non-canonical materials of the early 2nd century are varied and confusing. Thus we cannot say that the setting demanded by the GH is impossible, but the 2DH provides a more satisfactory solution of most of the problems.

[12] J. M. Robinson and H. Koester, *Trajectories through Early Christianity* (Philadelphia: Fortress, 1971) 232–68.

BIBLIOGRAPHY

Achtemeier, Paul J. "Toward the Isolation of Pre-Markan Miracle Cate-nae." *JBL* 89 (1970) 265-91.

_____. "The Origin and Function of the Pre-Markan Miracle Cate-nae." *JBL* 91 (1972) 198-221.

_____. *"Omne verbum sonat:* The New Testament and the Oral Envi-ronment of Late Antiquity." *JBL* 109 (1990) 3-27.

Bacon, B. W. *Studies in Matthew.* New York: Henry Holt, 1930.

Beare, F. W. "On the Synoptic Problem: A New Documentary Theory." *ATR* Supplemental Series 3 (1974) 15-28.

Bellinzoni, A. J. and others. *The Two-Source Hypothesis: A Critical Ap-praisal.* Macon, GA: Mercer University Press, 1965.

Benoit, P. and Boismard, M. E. *Synopse des quatre évangiles en français avec parallèles des apocryphes et des Pères.* Vol. 1, Paris: Cerf, 1965; Vol. 2, *Commentaires,* 1972.

Betz, H. D. "Jesus as Divine Man." *Jesus and the Historian.* Edited by F. T. Trotter; Philadelphia: Westminster, 1968.

_____. *Der Apostel Paulus und die sokratische Tradition.* Tübingen: J. C. B. Mohr, 1972.

_____. "The Literary Composition and Function of Paul's Letter to the Galatians." *NTS* 21 (1975) 353-79.

Bieler, L. *ΘΕΙΟΣ ΑΝΗΡ.* 2 vols. Darmstadt: Wissenschaftliche Buchgesell-schaft, 1967.

Black, Matthew. *An Aramaic Approach to the Gospels and Acts.* 3rd ed. Oxford: Clarendon Press, 1967.

Bornkamm, Günther. "Der Aufbau der Bergpredigt." *NTS* 24 (1978) 419-32.

Bornkamm, G., Barth, G. and Held, H. J. *Tradition and Interpretation in Matthew.* Philadelphia: Westminster, 1963.

Bousset, W. *Kyrios Christos.* Nashville: Abingdon, 1970.

Brooten, Bernadette. "Konnten Frauen im alten Judentum die Scheidung betreiben?" *EvT* 42 (1982) 65-80.

Brown, Raymond E. "The *Gospel of Peter* and Canonical Gospel Priority." *NTS* 33 (1987) 321-43.

Brown, R. E. and Meier, J. P. *Antioch and Rome.* New York: Paulist Press, 1983.

Buchanan, G. W. "Has the Griesbach Hypothesis Been Falsified?" *JBL* 93 (1972) 550-72.

Butler, B. C. *The Originality of St. Matthew.* Cambridge: Cambridge University Press, 1951.

Cadbury, Henry J. *The Making of Luke-Acts.* New York: Macmillan, 1927.

Carrington, Philip. *The Primitive Christian Calendar.* Cambridge: Cambridge University Press, 1952.

Collins, Adela Yarbro. "The Son of Man Sayings in the Sayings Source." *To Touch the Text: Biblical and Related Studies in Honor of J. A. Fitzmyer, S. J.* Edited by Maurya P. Horgan and Paul J. Kobelski. New York: Crossroad, 1989.

Conzelmann, Hans. *The Theology of St. Luke.* New York: Harper, 1960.

Cope, Lamar. "The Earliest Gospel was the Signs Gospel." *Jesus, the Gospels and the Church.* Edited by E. P. Sanders. Macon, GA: Mercer University Press, 1987.

Crossan, John Dominic. "Mark and the Relatives of Jesus." *NovT* 15 (1973) 81-113.

_____. *In Parables.* New York: Harper & Row, 1985.

Danker, F. W. *Luke.* Philadelphia: Fortress, 1976.

Daube, David. "Responsibilities of Master and Disciple in the Gospels." *NTS* 19 (1977) 1-15.

_____. "Four Types of Question." *JTS* n.s. 2 (1951) 45-48.

Dewey, Joanna. *Markan Public Debate: Literary Technique, Concentric Structure and Theology in Mark 2:1—3:6.* SBLDS 48. Chico, CA: Scholars Press, 1980.

Dibelius, Martin. *The Message of Jesus Christ.* New York: Scribners, 1939.

Dodd, C. H. *The Parables of the Kingdom.* 3rd ed. New York: Scribners, 1951.

Donahue, J. R. *The Gospel in Parable*. Philadelphia: Fortress, 1988.

Dowd, Sharyn Echols. *Prayer, Power, and the Problem of Suffering: Mark 11:22 in the Context of Marcan Theology*. Atlanta: Scholars Press, 1988.

Downing, F. G. "Towards the Rehabilitation of 'Q.'" *NTS* 11 (1965) 169-87.

Duling, D. C. "The Therapeutic Son of David: An Element in Matthew's Christological Apologetic." *NTS* 24 (1978) 398-410.

Dungan, D. L. "Reactionary Trends in the Gospel Producing Activity in the Early Church: Marcion, Tatian, Mark." *L'Evangile selon Marc, Tradition et Rédaction*. ed. M. Sabbe. Leuven: Leuven University Press, 1988.

Edwards, R. A. *A Theology of Q*. Philadelphia: Fortress, 1971.

Evans, C. F. "The Central Section in St. Luke's Gospel." *Studies in the Gospels*. Edited by D. E. Nineham. Oxford: Blackwell, 1955.

Farmer, W. R. *The Synoptic Problem: A Critical Analysis*. New York: Macmillan, 1964. 2nd ed., Dillsboro, NC: Western North Carolina Press, 1976.

_____. "Modern Developments of Griesbach's Hypothesis." *NTS* 23 (1977) 275-95.

_____. *Jesus and the Gospel*. Philadelphia: Fortress, 1982.

Farrer, A. M. "On Dispensing with Q." *Studies in the Gospels*. Edited by D. E. Nineham. Oxford: Blackwell, 1955.

Fortna, Robert T. *The Gospel of Signs*. Cambridge: Cambridge University Press, 1970.

_____. *The Fourth Gospel and Its Predecessors*. Philadelphia: Fortress, 1988.

Frye, Northrop. *Anatomy of Criticism*. Princeton: Princeton University Press, 1971.

_____. *The Great Code*. New York: Harcourt Brace Jovanovich, 1982.

Georgi, Dieter. *The Opponents of Paul in Second Corinthians*. Philadelphia: Fortress, 1986.

Grant, F. C. *The Gospels: Their Origin and Growth*. New York: Harper, 1957.

Haenchen, Ernst. "Die Komposition im Mk VIII:27—IX. 1." *NovT* 5 (1963) 81-109.

Havener, Ivan. *Q, the Sayings of Jesus.* Wilmington, DE: Michael Glazier, 1987.

Hobbs, Edward C. "A Quarter Century without Q." *Perkins Journal* 33.4 (Summer 1986) 10-19.

Honoré, A. M. "A Statistical Study of the Synoptic Problem." *NovT* 10 (1968) 95-147.

Jacobson, A. D. "The Literary Unity of Q." *JBL* 101 (1982) 365-89.

Johnson, S. E. *A Commentary on the Gospel according to St. Mark.* London: Black, 1977.

_____. "The Biblical Quotations in Matthew." *HTR* 36 (1943) 137-38.

_____. "Son of Man." *IDB* 4. 413-20.

_____. "The Davidic-Royal Motif in the Gospels." *JBL* 87 (1968) 140-43.

Kelber, W. H. *The Kingdom in Mark.* Philadelphia: Fortress, 1974.

_____. *The Oral and Wirtten Gospel.* Philadelphia: Fortress, 1983.

Kingsbury, Jack Dean. *The Parables of Jesus in Matthew 13.* Richmond: John Knox Press, 1969.

_____. *Matthew: Structure, Christology, Kingdom.* Philadelphia: Fortress, 1975.

_____. *The Christology of Mark's Gospel.* Philadelphia: Fortress, 1983.

_____. "The Religious Authorities in the Gospel of Mark." *NTS* 36 (1990) 42-65.

Kloppenborg, John S. *The Function of Q: Trajectories in Ancient Wisdom Collections.* Philadelphia: Fortress, 1987.

Knox, John. *Marcion and the New Testament.* Chicago: University of Chicago Press, 1942.

_____. "A Note on Mark 14:51-52." *The Joy of Study.* Edited by S. E. Johnson. New York: Macmillan, 1951.

_____. "Marcion's Gospel and the Synoptic Problem." *Jesus, the Gospels and the Church.* Edited by E. P. Sanders. Macon, GA: Mercer University Press, 1987.

Kurz, W. S. "Luke 3:28-38 and Greco-Roman and Biblical Genealogies." *Luke-Acts: New Perspectives from the Society of Biblical Literature Seminar*. Edited by C. H. Talbert. New York: Crossroad, 1984.

Lake, K. and Jackson, F. J. Foakes. *The Beginnings of Christianity. I. The Acts of the Apostles*. London: Macmillan, 1920.

Leaney, A. R. C. *The Gospel according to St. Luke*. London: Black, 1958.

Lightfoot, R. H. *History and Interpretation in the Gospels*. New York: Harper, 1935.

Lohmeyer, Ernst. *Das Evangelium des Markus*. Göttingen: Vandenhoeck & Ruprecht, 1959.

Lührmann, Dieter. "Die Pharisäer und die Schriftgelehrter im Markusevangelium." *ZNW* 78 (1987) 169-85.

_____. "The Gospel of Mark and the Sayings Collection Q." *JBL* 109 (1989) 169-85.

Malbon, Elizabeth Struthers. *Narrative Source and Mythic Meaning in Mark*. San Francisco: Harper & Row, 1986.

_____. "The Jesus of Mark and the Sea of Galilee." *JBL* 103 (1984) 363-77.

_____. "The Jewish Leaders in the Gospel of Mark: A Literary Study of Marcan Characterization." *JBL* 108 (1989) 259-87.

Marcus, Joel. *The Mystery of the Kingdom of God*. Atlanta: Scholars Press, 1986.

Marxsen, Willi. *Mark the Evangelist*. Nashville: Abingdon, 1969.

McCown, C. C. "The Geography of Luke's Central Section." *JBL* 57 (1938) 51-66.

Meagher, J. C. "Die Form- und Redaktionsungeschickliche Methoden: The Principle of Clumsiness and the Gospel of Mark." *JAAR* 43 (1975) 459-72.

_____. *Clumsy Construction in Mark's Gospel*. New York: Edwin Mellen, 1979.

Meeks, Wayne A. *The Prophet King*. Leiden: Brill, 1967.

Minear, Paul S. "Audience Criticism and Markan Eschatology." *Neues Testament und Geschichte*. Edited by H. Bartelsweiler and B. Reicke. Zürich and Tübingen: Gotthelf, 1972.

_____. "The Disciples and Crowds in the Gospel of Matthew." *ATR* Supplemental Series 3 (March 1974) 28-44.

Miyoshi, M. *Der Anfang des Reiseberichts Lk 9:51—10:24: eine redaktions-geschichtliche Untersuchung.* Rome: Pontifical Biblical Institute, 1974.

Montefiore, H. W. and Turner, H. E. W. *Thomas and the Evangelists.* Naperville, IL: Allenson, 1962.

Morgan, Donn F. *Between Text and Community.* Minneapolis: Augsburg, 1990.

Morgenthaler, Robert. *Statistische Synopse.* Zürich and Stuttgart: Gotthelf, 1971.

Murphy-O'Connor, Jerome. *The Holy Land.* Oxford: Oxford University Press, 1980.

Neirynck, F. with Theo Hansen and F. Van Segbroeck (eds.). *The Minor Agreements of Matthew and Luke against Mark with a Cumulative List.* BETL 39. Gembloux/Louvain: Duculot/Leuven University Press, 1974.

Parker, Pierson. *The Gospel before Mark.* Chicago: University of Chicago Press, 1953.

_____. "A Second Look at *The Gospel before Mark.*" *JBL* 100 (1981) 389-413.

Peabody, David B. *Mark as Composer.* Macon, GA: Mercer University Press, 1987.

Perrin, Norman. *Jesus and the Language of the Kingdom.* Philadelphia: Fortress, 1986.

_____. "Son of Man." *IDB* Suppl 633-35.

Perrin, N. and Duling, D. C. *The New Testament: An Introduction.* New York: Harcourt Brace Jovanovich, 1982.

Polag, Athanasius. *Fragmenta Q: Textheft zur Logienquelle.* Neukirchen-Vluyn: Neukirchener Verlag, 1979.

_____. *Die Christologie der Logienquelle.* NTAbh 8. Münster: Aschendorff, 1972.

Quesnell, Quentin. *The Mind of Mark.* Rome: Pontifical Biblical Institute, 1969.

Rice, George. "Western Non-Interpolations: A Defense of the Apostolate." *Luke-Acts: New Perspectives from the Society of Biblical Literature Seminar.* Edited by C. H. Talbert. New York: Crossroad, 1984.

Rieu, E. V. *The Four Gospels.* Baltimore: Penguin, 1953.

Robinson, J. A. T. "The Parable of the Wicked Husbandmen: a Test of Synoptic Relationships." *NTS* 11 (1975) 443-61.

Robinson, J. M. and Koester, H. *Trajectories through Early Christianity.* Philadelphia: Fortress, 1971.

Robinson, W. C., Jr. "The Theological Context for Interpreting Luke's Travel Narrative (9:51ff)." *JBL* 79 (1960) 20-31.

Saldarini, A. J. *Pharisees, Scribes and Sadducees in Palestinian Society: A Sociological Approach.* Wilmington, DE: Michael Glazier, 1988.

Schenk, Wolfgang. *Synopse zur Redenquelle der Evangelien: Q Synopse und Rekonstruktion in deutscher Übersetzung mit kurzen Erläuterungen.* Düsseldorf: Patmos, 1983.

Schmidt, K. L. *Der Rahmen der Geschichte Jesu.* Berlin: Trowitzsch, 1919.

_____. "Die Stellung der Evangelien in der allgemeinen Literaturgeschichte." *EYXAΡΙΣΤΗΡΙΟΝ.* Edited by H. Schmidt. Göttingen: Vandenhoeck & Ruprecht, 1923, Part 2.

Schreiber, Johannes. *Theologie des Vertrauens.* Hamburg: Porsche, 1967.

Schürmann, H. *Jesus und der Menschensohn.* Freiburg: Herder, 1975.

Sharman, H. B. *Son of Man and Kingdom of God.* New York: Harper, 1943.

Shepherd, M. H., Jr. *The Paschal Liturgy and the Apocalypse.* Richmond: John Knox Press, 1960.

Shuler, P. D. "The Genre of the Gospels and the Two Gospel Hypothesis." *Jesus, the Gospels and the Church.* Edited by E. P. Sanders. Macon, GA: Mercer University Press, 1987.

Smith, Morton. "The Aretalogy Used by Mark." *The Aretalogy Used by Mark: Protocol of the Sixth Colloquy of the Center for Hermeneutical Studies in Hellenistic and Modern Culture.* Edited by W. Wuellner. Berkeley, CA: Center for Hermeneutical Studies, 1978.

_____. "Prolegomena to a Discussion of Aretalogies, Divine Men, the Gospels, and Jesus." *JBL* 90 (1971) 174-99.

Stendahl, Krister. "Matthew." *PCB,* 769-98.

Strack, H. L. and Billerbeck, P. *Kommentar zum Neuen Testament aus Talmud und Midrasch.* Munich: C. H. Beck, 1922.

Styler, G. M. "The Priority of Mark." *The Birth of the New Testament.* Edited by C. F. D. Moule. London: Black, 1962.

Talbert, Charles H. *Literary Patterns, Theological Themes, and the Genre of Luke-Acts.* Missoula, MT: Scholars Press, 1974.

_____. *What is a Gospel?* Philadelphia: Fortress, 1977.

Talbert, C. H. and McKnight, E. V. "Can the Griesbach Hypothesis Be Falsified?" *JBL* 91 (1972) 338-68.

Tannehill, R. C. "The Disciples in Mark." *JR* 57 (1977) 386-405.

Taylor, Vincent. "The Original Order of Q." *New Testament Essays in Memory of T. W. Manson.* Edited by A. J. B. Higgins. Manchester: Manchester University Press, 1959.

Theissen, Gerd. *Sociology of Early Christianity.* Philadelphia: Fortress, 1978.

Thysman, Raymond. *Communauté et directives éthiques: la catéchèse de Matthieu.* Gembloux: Duculot, 1974.

Tuckett, C. M. *The Revival of the Griesbach Hypothesis: An Analysis and Appraisal.* Cambridge: Cambridge University Press, 1983.

Tyson J. B. "The Two-Source Hypothesis: A Critical Appraisal." *The Two-Source Hypothesis: A Critical Appraisal.* Edited by A. J. Bellinzoni and others. Macon, GA: Mercer University Press, 1965.

_____. "Scripture, Torah and Sabbath in Luke-Acts." *Jesus, the Gospels and the Church.* Edited by E. P. Sanders. Macon, GA: Mercer University Press, 1987.

Vielhauer, Philipp. "Gottesreich und Menschensohn in der Verkündigung Jesu." *Aufsätze zum Neuen Testament.* Munich: C. Kaiser, 1955.

Votaw, C. W. "The Gospels and Contemporary Biographies." *AJT* 19 (1915) 45-73, 217-49.

Waetjen, H. N. "The Ending of Mark and the Gospel's Shift in Eschatology." *Journal of the Swedish Theological Institute* 4 (1965) 114-31.

Weeden, T. J. *Mark—Traditions in Conflict.* Philadelphia: Fortress, 1971.

Wegner, Judith Romney. *Chattel or Property? The Status of Women in the Mishnah.* Oxford: Oxford University Press, 1988.

Wilamowitz, Ulrich von. *Kultur der Gegenwart,* cited in J. Weiss, *Earliest Christianity.* Vol. 2. New York: Harper, 1958.

Wilder, Amos N. *The Language of the Gospel: Early Christian Rhetoric.* New York: Harper & Row, 1964.

Wilkinson, John. *Egeria's Travels in the Holy Land.* Rev. ed. Jerusalem: Ariel, 1981.

Wuellner, Wilhelm. "Greek Rhetoric and Pauline Argumentation." *Early Christian Literature and the Classical Intellectual Tradition.* Edited by W. R. Schoedel and R. L. Wilken. Paris: Beauchesne, 1977.

INDEX OF PASSAGES

INDEX OF SUBJECTS

169

INDEX OF MODERN AUTHORS

171